HARNESS YOUR BUTTERFLIES

THE YOUNG PROFESSIONAL'S
METAMORPHOSIS
TO AN EXCITING CAREER

Copyright © 2020 Benjamin Preston
All rights reserved. No part of this publication may be reproduced, distributed, or transmitted in any form or by any means, including photocopying, recording, or other electronic or mechanical methods, without the prior written permission of the publisher, except in the case of brief quotations embodied in critical reviews and certain other noncommercial uses permitted by copyright law. For permission requests, write to the publisher, addressed "Attention: Permissions Coordinator," at the address below.

www.benjaminpreston.com

ISBN: 978-1-7346081-0-6 (print)
ISBN: 978-1-7346081-1-3 (ebook)

Ordering Information:
Special discounts are available on quantity purchases by corporations, associations, and others. For details, contact Benjamin@benjaminpreston.com.

CONTENTS

CHAPTER 1:	Harnessing Your Butterflies	1
CHAPTER 2:	Transforming Anxious Energy into Personal Power	9
CHAPTER 3:	When to Give Up (And When to Give Your All)	17
CHAPTER 4:	Six Months of Intentional Action Will Put You Five Years Ahead	27
CHAPTER 5:	Puzzle-Piece Strengths	35
CHAPTER 6:	What's Your Hot Button?	47
CHAPTER 7:	Canada: The 51st State	55
CHAPTER 8:	No Cell Phones at the Dinner Table	63
CHAPTER 9:	The Diamond Effect	73
CHAPTER 10:	Be Like Mike	83
CHAPTER 11:	Speaking Doesn't Help You Understand	91
CHAPTER 12:	The Single Secret to Team Success	99
CHAPTER 13:	The Lost Art of Conciseness	107
CHAPTER 14:	The Cowardly Lion	113
CHAPTER 15:	The More Lives You Live, The More Empathy You Gain	119
CHAPTER 16:	The Real "You"	127
CHAPTER 17:	Quarter-Life Crisis	137
CHAPTER 18:	Impact Starts with You	145
	Epilogue	153

BENJAMIN PRESTON

HARNESS YOUR BUTTERFLIES

THE YOUNG PROFESSIONAL'S
METAMORPHOSIS
TO AN EXCITING CAREER

CHAPTER 1
Harnessing Your Butterflies

Do you wake up and dread going to work? Do you lie in bed wondering if you should get dressed, call in sick, or just quit?

Looking back at your choices that led you to this job, was this the job you were supposed to take? Is it a stepping-stone to something better? Why doesn't it excite you? Is it just a dead end?

Many of us struggle to find happiness in our careers for a myriad of reasons, and most of the time, we're not confident enough to make the change we desperately crave. If you're like me, you were taught from a young age to follow your passions, but then you found your passions don't always pay the bills. So, you're stuck at a crossroads.

Now, not only do you lack confidence in your career path, but you're experiencing one of the most uncertain employment eras in history due to big data, AI, automation, etc. Is your job going to be outsourced to a computer? Where will your business be in the next five years and will you still be needed?

I felt this exact tension and stress in my own career.

I started my career working for a large, multinational communications company as an entry-level communications associate. Still unsure of what I really wanted to do, I explored various disciplines within my role—public relations, advertising, marketing, human resources, culture, corporate social responsibility, and more.

Still feeling that I wasn't making an impact, I jumped to a small startup where I oversaw marketing. Although I was making a direct impact on our team and the product, I didn't feel that my impact actually mattered.

So, I moved jobs again, this time to a Native American economic development firm directing a marketing department across more than 40 subsidiary companies. While I was making a significant social impact, I questioned if I was doing what I loved.

By the time I was 27, I had obtained my MBA and had experience in several industries including healthcare, marketing, SaaS (Software as a Service), architecture, consulting, real estate, retail, wholesale distribution, manufacturing, and government contracting. With all this experience and education, I still feared what the future of my career would be. I was like a leaf blowing in the wind, and I hoped I'd end up somewhere favorable. I spent many years trying to develop myself so I could prepare for the future. But in that time, I learned our careers are completely within our control, even if it doesn't feel like it right now.

Throughout this book, I will share the wisdom I have discovered along my journey that has allowed me to reclaim my power and create a career I'm excited about. With every step we take together, you will discover new ways of looking at the world and new skills you can apply to your development. By the end, you will have the necessary interpersonal skills to mold yourself into a well-rounded leader, confidently embrace the future, and create the career you've always wanted—one that gives you butterflies.

The saying "butterflies in your stomach" is a clever way of explaining how our bodies experience excitement (or nervousness), and I've always found it to be an interesting concept.

When you hear "butterflies in your stomach," you may think back to a time of extreme panic or nervousness. Having butterflies in your stomach makes your heart stop, because it means you're about to do something terrifying, such as public speaking or talking to your crush for the first time. But that sensation goes so much deeper than sweaty palms and a dry mouth.

Scientifically, the fluttering you feel is your body pumping blood away from your gut to other areas of your body. It's preparing you for a fight-or-flight response. Then you may start to feel tingling and jittering in your legs, fingers, and brains. The sensation of excitement and nervousness, biologically speaking, is the same sensation.

"Fear and excitement are the exact same physical state," says Mel Robbins in one of her inspirational YouTube videos.[1] "The only difference between fear and excitement is what your brain is doing while your body is all agitated."

In other words, excitement and nervousness are labels for the same sensation. You're about to embark on a journey to create an exciting career. At times, you will be nervous or scared. Embrace that feeling, and label it as excitement.

Having butterflies in your stomach is your body's way of telling you that you're outside your comfort zone. From now on, what we will call excitement is a full-body response that starts with a small fluttering in our stomachs. If you feel butterflies, it's a sign that you're moving in the right direction.

Comedian Jim Carrey gave an amazing analogy during a commencement speech to a Maharishi University of Management[2] graduating class that summarizes this point perfectly. He said:

> *My father could have been a great comedian, but he didn't believe that that was possible for him, and so he made a conservative choice. Instead, he got a safe job as an accountant. And when I was 12 years old, he was let go from that safe job, and our family had to do whatever we could to survive.*
>
> *I learned many great lessons from my father, not the*

---

[1] Mel Robbins, "The Secret to Stopping Fear and Anxiety (That Actually Works)," February 8, 2017, video, 12:24, https://www.youtube.com/watch?v=6n8i7ua0mSw.

[2] Jim Carrey, "Full Speech: Jim Carrey's Commencement Address at the 2014 MUM Graduation…," May 30, 2014, video, 26:08, https://www.youtube.com/watch?v=V80-gPkpH6M.

least of which was that: You can fail at what you don't want, so you might as well take a chance on doing what you love.

Carrey's father isn't unique in this approach; most of us live our lives that way. Fear usually stops us from pursuing careers that excite us—fear of risk and failure. And that fear often stems from this phrase we all learn at a young age: *supposed to*.

I'm *supposed to* go to college. I'm *supposed to* find a stable job in a high-paying industry. I'm *supposed to* pick a career field early and stick with it. *Supposed to* can keep us safe and stable, but it never satisfies us.

You may invest time in building your career without really knowing what you want to do—all because of the words *supposed to*. I moved forward with my career based on where I thought I was *supposed to* go—whether the butterflies were present or not.

As you're reading this book, you likely have a goal in mind. Maybe you're a college student wondering which career or major to choose. Or, you're a fresh graduate scared to go out into the world because you feel unprepared. Maybe you're a young professional feeling stuck or unsure about your future.

No matter where you are in your professional journey, one of the first interpersonal lessons you must learn to be successful is to be excited about your career. The happiness you feel in your position matters. Your excitement to get up and go to work matters. Your optimism for the future matters.

So, assuming you're still reading this, I'm guessing you don't have those butterflies about your career yet. And that's ok. No matter where you are right now, remember that you are *never* stuck. Let me emphasize that: *You are never stuck.*

Take the pressure off yourself to get it 100-percent right. You'll have times when you will feel stuck and times where you feel in the zone. As you grow throughout this book, you'll find that each chapter will elevate your confidence little by little, and you will understand how you can move forward in the right direction. You'll discover you have the necessary skills to succeed.

At the beginning of my career, I felt unprepared for the future. The lessons and advice I'm going to share with you are the lessons I've learned along my journey. These lessons improved my confidence and reassured me that I had the power to create an exciting career for myself.

You might already feel a little lighter than when you first started this chapter. Sink into that light feeling. As you imagine your future passion-filled career, you should feel butterflies. You can use your butterflies as a benchmark, and you won't settle for anything less.

Imagine building your perfect career like you're playing a game of darts. You start with the goal to hit the bullseye of a perfect career—the tiny red dot smack-dab in the middle. Circled around the bullseye are several other possible point values, some worth more than others. Many of us play darts never expecting to hit the bullseye, so we hope to hit something above 15 if we can't get the perfect 50. Better to get some points than none, right?

We throw our first dart, and it flies way off. We adjust slightly. We throw the next one and get a little closer. We keep trying until, ideally, we get that 50-point bullseye. But, many of us just hope for something above zero.

From this point forward, our butterflies will indicate we're scoring 50. As you grow and develop your career, you'll have the opportunity to go for 50 or settle for 15. We're going to use our butterflies to get us as close to perfect as we can get.

As you choose excitement over fear, your overall happiness will improve. You'll also be more efficient in your role, because job performance is directly connected to how happy and excited you are to do it.

As you move forward through this book, be open to challenging your previous conceptions of *supposed to* and remember the career you crave is completely within reach. While at times the exercises and advice will push you out of your comfort zone, it's important to remember that the investment in your growth will serve as a strong foundation on which you can build your dream career.

CHAPTER 2
Transforming Anxious Energy into Personal Power

What am I *supposed to* do with my life?

You search for the right job at the right company that will put you on the right career path. Then, you overthink those career paths and question if they align with what you're *meant* to do. Does this job align with your life purpose? Better yet, what is your life purpose?

Purpose-driven questions often cause us to get stuck when we look for jobs or career paths—especially early on in our careers. Our culture has hardwired us to always stretch for more, but in doing so, we often focus too much on the *destination* instead of the journey. And when we talk about life purpose, we are coded to believe that it's one destination that we will someday reach—except that's not how it works. If we solely focus on our future life purpose, we forget to enjoy the journey and to live our purpose *today*.

Purpose isn't a destination we reach tomorrow; it's a conscious feeling that happens today—a feeling of impact, fulfillment, and gratitude. Instead of chasing destiny's moving target, we need to turn our ambition to something more tangible to get that feeling of impact, fulfillment, and gratitude.

A literary framework created by Joseph Campbell in his book *The Hero with a Thousand Faces* explains this perfectly. It's called the hero's journey. Many classic stories share this framework—the *Odyssey, Alice in Wonderland, Star Wars, Harry Potter,* etc.

The framework is basic. First, the protagonist is called to adventure. They initially decline the call to adventure, but a pivot point (the death of a loved one, a prophecy, etc.) forces them to pursue the journey. They often set out with one purpose in mind, but they don't have the tools yet to succeed. They go through trials and tribulations. All the while, their journey becomes more complicated and problematic. Eventually the protagonist accomplishes their mission and becomes a hero.

If you put yourself in the shoes of the hero, you, too, are called to adventure. Whenever you see new opportunities and feel excited, that's the call to adventure. Some of you may have experienced this call already. But, more likely, you're thinking, "I have never been called to *adventure*."

Often in reality, adventures aren't glamourous and surrounded by fanfare. No one is going to announce them to you. The call to adventure comes in the form of impulses. When you stop looking for the giant sign that says "Life Purpose Turn Left" and start noticing the subtle feelings of butterflies, you'll be well on your way to adventure.

While finding your adventure is important, the real purpose of your life lies in the journey, not the destination. Heroes aren't remembered for their glamorized heroes' returns. They're remembered for their grit and adventure on the journey that make them successful. For example:

- Hercules isn't remembered for becoming a god. He's celebrated for his 12 trials that allowed him to become a god.

- Alice's story wouldn't be nearly as interesting if we just looked at the beginning and end. The enjoyment of her story lies in the chaos and whimsy of her adventures in Wonderland.

- Harry Potter's relevance isn't for killing Voldemort. Instead, an entire entertainment empire is built around his journey—well before he killed the Dark Lord.

The point is, we're fixated on reaching the end of our stories and building our lives around that outcome. Instead, we should be looking at what trials and challenges can engage us as we go toward our destination. If we arrive at our destination without contrast, we will never feel fulfilled. It's more gratifying to read the whole book than just the first and last chapter.

Life's Purpose or More Purposeful Life

In order to truly live purposefully, we need to change the purpose questions that we ask. So, where do we start?

First, we need to retire the question, "What is my life purpose?" and begin asking the question, "What will make my life more purposeful today?"

What will make our lives more purposeful today? Opportunities are all around us, but from where we stand now, it may seem like we're extremely limited in our options. To help shine a light on our available opportunities, we need to take a small step back. Let's start with how we determine purpose at work. Individuals experience purposeful work in two ways, according to a study published in 2015 by Personality and Social Psychology Bulletin.[3]

First is a fluid belief in purpose: "I can find meaning in any career." Individuals who fall into this group tend to stay with jobs longer because they find their jobs fulfilling. Second is a fixed belief in purpose: "I have one purpose, and my goal is to find it." Individuals who belong to this group flutter from job to job until they find the right one. I think of these categories as bookends to a career-purpose spectrum.

Strategies for Both Types

I've created some strategies based on this research that will allow you to confidently take your next step into living a purposeful life, starting with two approaches. Both approaches require the use of your internal guidance

---

[3] Patricia Chen, Phoebe Ellsworth, and Norbert Schwarz, "Finding a Fit or Developing It: Implicit Theories About Achieving Passion for Work," *Personality and Social Psychology Bulletin*, October 2015.

system—your butterflies.

The first approach, Career Strategist, focuses on finding and creating opportunities based on intended strategies you hope to learn along your journey. This approach is useful for people who say, "I know what I want. I'm open to learning and I believe specific opportunities will strongly benefit my career."

CAREER STRATEGISTS

Career Strategists can love any job if they put their minds to it. In this approach, finding a career-path opportunity requires more of an introspective search with external validation from trusted advisors.

Discovery

If you're a Career Strategist, you typically look for a career function/industry and search for job titles within. When searching for career paths, you may take an inventory of careers and industries you're drawn to. If you begin thinking of an industry and you feel butterflies, you're headed in the right direction.

Defining the Journey

The journey provides fulfillment. Before you create your end point, you can outline what you would like to learn from the journey that will make your life purposeful today.

For example, Carrie loves the healthcare industry. She gets butterflies at the idea of understanding and articulating the mysteries of the human body. She loves being able to provide counseling to sick individuals and see them get better. Recently, she's discovered that she enjoys a fast-paced environment.

Narrowing Opportunities

Once you get more pieces in place for your journey, you will see more clearly what you're excited about and if it's sustainable. Now you need to narrow your focus within your industry.

As you narrow your focus, begin to research the structure of that industry. If you're looking at the health industry, for example, start to understand the branches of work that support the human body. You could work in medicine, physical therapy, nutrition, etc. Begin to narrow three or four specific arenas that spark excitement without sacrificing your journey.

If you're still not completely sure if the industry you've selected is right for you, that's okay. If you feel excited about the opportunities you've selected, that's enough.

CAREER EXPERIMENTERS

The second approach, Career Experimenters, focuses on sifting opportunities through a metaphorical "swipe right, swipe left" mentality. This approach is useful for people who say, "I know what I don't want, but I'm open to learning what I do want. I will continue refining what I want as I go."

Discovery

If you're a Career Experimenter, the discovery process will be a little lengthier than for Career Strategists because you have more content to sift through.

First, make a list of things you enjoy. These can be hard skills (writing, speaking, etc.), soft skills (influencing, creativity, etc.), or past experiences. Jot down 50 or so items. You can search online if you need some ideas.

Once you've developed the list, review it. Highlight the nonnegotiables, the things that make your butterflies flutter. For example, you may be a great communicator, academically gifted, and strong at influencing others.

Defining the Journey

As a Career Experimenter, your journey definition may be more fluid because of your nature. You may fumble around with identifying what you like and don't like, and that's your guide. As you define your journey, you'll need to be more general, so get creative with it. You may have to write several journey points before you start feeling the butterflies.

For example, Brandon is a good communicator, so he may want to find a career that allows him to communicate using various formats such as visual, written, and digital. Or, since he's academically gifted, he may want to explore a career that uses frameworks and research when developing solutions.

Narrowing Opportunities

As you start to consider careers that interest you, look for roles with flexibility and mobility. You can either develop a list of specific roles or you can list larger functional verticals.

If you've identified that you're a good communicator, you may want to look at specific roles such as copywriter, public relations specialist, and journalist. You can also look at wider functional verticals, like communications, marketing, or business development, that have several career paths within them.

The goal is to identify opportunities that spark excitement. Whether you are a recent college grad or a working professional looking for a change, these approaches will allow you to narrow your effort to secure the opportunity you want.

While you still may be anxious to know your purpose, the road along your journey is filled with learning and beauty. Take the time to enjoy the path you're on today and make that road purposeful now. Start asking, "What will make my life more purposeful today?" and the answers you uncover will guide you to your life purpose.

CHAPTER 3
When to Give Up (And When to Give Your All)

Have you ever started reading a book, gotten halfway through, then stopped? Or you say you want six-pack abs, then pay for a yearly gym membership that you never use?

If you're anything like me, you have a bookshelf of half-read books, and you skipped the gym again today. It's not from a lack of wanting; it's from a lack of motivation. Your motivation isn't in line with your goals.

Motivation plays a critical role in our lives. It's the reason we start, continue, and maintain habits (or don't). For professionals, successfully tapping and sustaining motivation is the difference between creating an exciting career or falling into a dead end.

In this chapter, you are going to explore the psychology of motivation, discover your true motives, and learn how to hack your motivation when you want to reach your goals.

Think of your career as the unused gym membership. You have a clear goal in mind, and the thought of six-pack abs gives you butterflies. You hit the gym with some intensity. After a couple weeks, your excitement starts to wear off. You show up and go through the motions, and after a while, you make up excuses for why you can't work out. After a couple months, your goal becomes too difficult, or you let other obstacles get in the way of your workouts, and you stop going to the gym.

As professionals we can relate to this analogy, because it's comparable to our experience when we start a new job. We get excited to start but the butterflies quickly fade. Work becomes a chore. This is because our motivation to chase an opportunity is not the same motivation that we use to do the actual work.

Discovering your motivations is a personal experience, but one that can be better understood through two popular theories, *Maslow's hierarchy of needs* and the *achievement motivation theory*.

Maslow's hierarchy of needs identifies five levels of human needs, starting from basic to complex. Our fundamental need for survival motivates us to seek shelter, food, and water. As we move up the pyramid of needs, we are motivated to seek love and affirmation from those around us because of an instinctual need to be accepted.

Maslow's framework helps us understand basic needs and the importance of animalistic instincts in accomplishing our goals, but as working professionals, animalistic instincts don't always motivate us to attend meetings or create budgets. Other theories like the achievement motivation theory suggest that humans have one of three motivations: achievement, affiliation, or power. This theory suggests that each person has a primary motivation to achieve goals, affiliate with others, or have power.

The achievement motivation theory gives more insight into our professional minds, but often we have more than one motivation for doing something. Further, we usually don't have that one motivation consistently through the entire process of initiation, guidance, and maintenance.

Both theories give us a glimpse into the breadth of what motivates us to act. To uncover our unique motivations, we need to understand our needs and wants.

Jeffrey S. Nevid, professor of psychology at St. John's University, defines motivation as the process that initiates, guides, and maintains goal-oriented behaviors.[4]

1. Initiation—our ability to start something

2. Guidance—the vigor and concentration we put into accomplishing our goal

3. Maintenance—our ability to stick with something

A unique combination of needs and wants could underlie these three components.

Various motivational frameworks say initiation could serve both our needs and wants. For example, we decide to start a gym membership. Our "want" may be to have a

---

[4] My Linh Nguyen, "The Impact of Employees [sic] Motivation on Organizational Effectiveness," abstract (thesis, Vaassan Ammattikorkeakoulu University of Applied Sciences, 2017), https://pdfs.semanticscholar.org/389f/f8eda5e7cf25ae8b598eb28ff81a1ae017bc.pdf.

six pack. Our "need" may be that we're seeking acceptance from our partner. Both are equally important but not altogether sustainable.

Another example may be searching for a new job. We "want" to challenge our skills and grow our knowledge base. Our "need" might be a bigger paycheck to pay off our massive student debt. Both motivations are valid. After a couple months of having a new job, those motivations will change, and we'll need to be ready for that.

Guidance is connected to our excitement about the goal and our ability (strengths and weaknesses) to execute it. Going back to our gym example, perhaps we are starting to see results, and we're excited to use those results as our motivation. Or, maybe our motivation has changed. Now that we're starting to work out, maybe we begin training for a specific event like a marathon. And, as a result, we've gamified our experience and we look forward to going to the gym.

The professional motivation to work with more vigor and better concentration might, for example, be connected to our strengths and weaknesses. We may need to exert better concentration to understand a critical element of our job. Or, we may exert more vigor toward a project if we're excited about it and it naturally aligns with our strengths. In both cases, our underlying motivation might be more than just money to pay bills as it was in the initiation phase.

Our drive for maintenance is often attached to a specific goal or outcome. Motivation that accompanies maintenance must be strong enough to withstand inevitable obstacles. For example, if we want six-pack abs, we will have to withstand the challenges of core workouts—no matter how awful they are.

Let's look at a professional example of how this might work. Our initiating motivation was to get a bigger paycheck. And now that we're working toward a promotion or new job, we find ourselves getting competitive with our coworkers. We are no longer motivated solely by a bigger paycheck; we're motivated by winning the coveted promotion. Our maintaining motivation is competition, which can be an animalistic instinct.

Uncover Your Motivations

Use these questions to help you uncover your unique motivations:

Initiation

Which "needs" does this new opportunity fill?
Which "wants" will this opportunity fill?
Who do you want to impress by doing this? Why?
Why choose this opportunity over something else?
What are you seeking from this opportunity?
Could you substitute this opportunity for something else? Why not?
Is this opportunity risky? Is that why you're pursuing it?

Guidance

Is your motivation the same as initiation?

How much intensity are you putting into this opportunity?
How much concentration are you putting into this opportunity?
Are you able to keep the pace of operating like you have been?
Does this opportunity align with your strengths?
Is it fun?

Maintenance
Why do you want to keep working on this?
Is this harder or easier than you thought?
Do you enjoy the work?
What is this work helping you to accomplish?
What else are you learning from this opportunity?
Is this opportunity still accomplishing your original goal?
Has your goal changed?

If you find yourself in a situation where you are unexcited about the motivation, you can hack that motivation to make it more exciting and sustainable. For example, if you're required to take classes for a work certification, you can turn your motivation from a need into a want to make it more exciting.

Strategies to Help You Hack Your Motivations

Let's spice up your motivations with some of these strategies.

1. Change your perspective from need to want

The first strategy to hacking your motivation is to shift your perspective. Usually, if you find yourself dragging on a goal, it's because you're telling yourself an unhelpful story. To combat that, change the story to something that's a little more exciting.

Let's say you are working toward a promotion. Your current motivation may be to earn more money, which means you're focusing on the lack of money you currently have. Your story, then, might be that you're desperate for money and can't move forward without more money.

Being desperate for money is not motivating. It feels more like a trap than anything. Let's change the story to be a little more upbeat with the same goal in mind.

You've learned so much from your current role. This promotion could be another opportunity for you to continue your learning. You're open to growth and mobility, and with a promotion, you'd be able to work on cool projects you've always admired.

Can you feel the difference? Learning is a lot more exciting than being desperate for money. The shift went from "I need money" to "I want to learn." Typically, shifting motivations from needs to wants puts you more in control. If you need something, you're dependent on that outcome. If you want something, you can continually shift your motivation until it gives you butterflies.

2. Align to a bigger purpose

Another strategy to shift your motivation is to align it to a bigger purpose. This could either be a bigger purpose that you develop or an organizational purpose that you agree with.

For example, you might dread going to work every day because your job is boring. So instead of looking at your motivation as something as basic as "this job allows me to pay off student debt," look at it through the lens of a bigger purpose.

Let's say your job is a project manager for a professional services company. Your company services large clients, and it pays well. Your main client sells soda. Your bigger picture might be that you're a critical team member for moving projects forward. Without you, your client wouldn't be able to sell soda.

In the even bigger picture, your work allows families to come together and celebrate special occasions. Your skills give people an extra boost of energy to get through the rest of their day. Or, you allow customers to enjoy their "cheat day" in a relaxing way.

Those scenarios ladder up to a larger purpose. If your motivation is altruistic, you'll be more excited to show up to work to project manage soda campaigns.

3. Give up

Sometimes a lack of motivation is an indicator that you've reached a natural exit point. It's okay to acknowledge that, but make sure you're not leaving because it's hard.

I once worked on a SaaS product, but after a while, my motivation to work on the project was dwindling because it was no longer shiny or flashy. It seemed dull to me. So, I tried making it fun. I tried aligning it to a bigger purpose.

I even tried using animalistic instinct as motivation, but nothing worked. Eventually, I weighed my options and decided to seek a new opportunity.

If you do decide to give up, do it with integrity and the right intentions. Overall, understanding your motivation and manipulating it (when necessary) will allow you to accomplish your goals more efficiently. Whether you're looking to shift motivation for initiation, guidance, or maintenance, hacking your motives will allow you to go from boring to exciting relatively easy.

As you continue to grow professionally, you will be able to uncover your true motivations a lot quicker and hack them when needed. Make sure your motivations give you butterflies, and if your motivations don't make you excited, hack them.

CHAPTER 4

Six Months of Intentional Action Will Put You Five Years Ahead

A simple technique could save you years of hustling—and help you accomplish your goal within six months.

By being *intentional* with how you spend your time, you will be able to expedite your time to exceed your goals. And, part of being intentional means clearly defining your goals before you start the grind and maintaining boundaries to keep your intentions intact while you work.

You're probably intentional with a lot of things in your life—where you spend your money, which causes you support, etc. But you may not be intentional with how you invest in your career.

Early in my career, I wanted to make a huge impact and prove my worth to everybody—my team, our execs, and our clients. I was in an entry-level position with aspirations to make it to the top. So, I started hustling. I took on project after project, stacking jobs on my plate like I was at a buffet.

After a couple months, I felt like I was drowning.

I invested the bulk of my time in high-visibility jobs because I didn't want to disappoint our executives, so my day-to-day work began to suffer. I wasn't helping my team. I wasn't helping our execs. And I couldn't help our clients.

This *burnout* is common for many professionals. In a 2018 study by Gallup, two-thirds of full-time workers experience burnout on the job.[5] We're taught to hustle, but we don't set a direction for ourselves. We build unintentional careers by overextending to unexciting things.

As Americans, we love that feeling of being overly "busy" because it gives us a false sense of importance. We equate busyness with success—even the word "busyness" is one letter away from "business." Therefore, if our professional intention is to be successful, then we need to be busy.

A research article titled "Conspicuous Consumption of Time: When Busyness and Lack of Leisure Time Become a Status Symbol" looks at why busyness and success are mistakenly equated.[6] The report says that professionals gain status by becoming unavailable or scarce. This status is "…driven by the perceptions that a busy person possesses desired human capital characteristics (e.g.,

---

[5] Ben Wigert and Sangeeta Agrawal, "Employee Burnout, Part 1: The 5 Main Causes," *Gallup*, July 12, 2018, https://www.gallup.com/workplace/237059/employee-burnout-part-main-causes.aspx.

[6] Silvia Bellezza, Neeru Paharia, Anat Keinen, "Conspicuous Consumption of Time: When Busyness and Lack of Leisure Time Become a Status Symbol," *Journal of Consumer Research*, December 27, 2016, https://academic.oup.com/jcr/article/44/1/118/2736404.

competence and ambition) and is scarce and in demand in the job market."

This shows basic supply and demand. Since demand for our talents is so high, it must mean that we're extremely valuable. Or, so we think.

This report also found that social media plays a role in perpetuating this false narrative. In an experiment, researchers posted on behalf of "Sally" to make her look busy, and they studied people's perceptions of her.

"As expected, participants found Sally in the busy-Facebook-posts condition to possess higher human capital characteristics and to be more scarce and in demand," they concluded.

Why does Sally's experiment matter?

We buy into this idea that we are valuable, which is why we need to be in demand. Except, our valuation is determined by others—how in demand other people think we are. We need to flip that valuation. Our value should come from us, and how we determine our worth.

Do you think you're valuable?

If the answer is yes, then you most likely actively decide where your time should be spent. That's the core of intentionality.

Once you realize your true value, you start to question why you're wasting your time with things that don't give you butterflies. When you think you're valuable, you evaluate your intentions and realign them with what you want to do.

And, as you invest in your priorities, you will expedite the time it takes to accomplish your personal and professional goals. You will be able to focus your effort on what matters and drop everything else. What you do with your time matters, so it's time to be intentional with your work.

When you're starting out in your career, your intentions might be vague and broad. As you advance, your intentions become more focused and more impactful. Two elements of intentionality will allow you to focus more clearly and achieve the outcome you're seeking—to help you achieve your goals within six months.

The first is getting clear on your goal and your purpose for that goal.

The second is setting hard boundaries and reinforcing them.

Get Clear on Your Goals

Once you've stated your intentions clearly, the process of reaching your goals will flow naturally and make more sense. Think of an intention as the purpose you're assigning to your work. Your intention might be to learn new technical skills that will make you more valuable in your field. Or, you may want to improve the client experience. Or, you may want to create a more engaging work culture.

When setting intentions, you can get creative with how you want to make an impact. You'll be surprised; in most work environments, your supervisors will be more than happy to accommodate your intentionality. (A small word to the wise, be sure to job sculpt your role in partnership with your supervisor instead of behind their back.)

From a professional standpoint, your goals should always be timely, measurable, and action-oriented. Some programs will teach goal setting differently, but SMART goals are usually a good place to start.

S – Specific
M – Measurable
A – Achievable/Attainable
R – Relevant
T – Time Bound

Instead of aimlessly taking on tons of projects as I did, narrow your focus: "I want to create a more engaging customer experience." If I had done that, it would have immediately narrowed down my overall project list so I could more efficiently develop goals. For example:

- Create a mobile-first website by EOY to host our company news and awards.
- Develop an email marketing plan by June to promote upcoming incentives.
- Conduct customer surveys every quarter.

These three projects immediately move the needle on improving the customer experience, which was my intention.

You can get bogged down as a professional by oversaturating yourself with new goals. When you begin to create your goals, develop two or three anchor points and let everything else start to fade into the background.

If you're in a team setting where you cannot fade items into the background, talk to your team about it. Your new intention might be to sculpt your role in a way that allows you to grow. A process like job sculpting, or the act of developing a customized career path within your role, may be a good strategy to implement as you become more intentional.

The process of fading and job sculpting won't happen overnight, but over a period of six months, you will have reached your dream state. Being upfront and intentional will give you the experience and support you'll need so you won't have to wait five years to be where you want to be.

In this new state, you will also be able to focus your energy on tasks and projects that matter to you. That focused investment will go a long way.

Set Hard Boundaries (and Keep Them)

The second half of intentionality is establishing and reinforcing hard boundaries. Your boundaries are the things you tolerate (or don't). In a physical sense, you know exactly what maintaining boundaries feels like. If someone is standing uncomfortably close to you, you will either take a step back or ask them for space.

Professionally, maintaining boundaries is a little

murkier. Once you've created your intentions, maintaining boundaries becomes easier. Every task or project should either fit or not fit your intention. If it doesn't fit, don't do it.

For my example, after hustling and hustling with diminished returns, I decided to be intentional about my work. So, instead of working on 20 projects, I worked on five that matched my focus.

Maintaining boundaries isn't always easy. But eventually you will be able to look at any project to determine if it expands your technical skills or not. If a project doesn't fit within your intention, don't do it.

In some professional settings, it can be challenging to say no—and in some cases you're saddled with assigned responsibilities outside of your focus. It's important to be up front with your supervisor about your intentions, and to diminish your input as much as you can on energy-sapping projects that are outside of your focus. At times, your intention may not align with your role, and you will need to use discretion with whom you share your intentions.

Stating your intention clearly will allow you to focus your career for expedited growth. By investing six months of constant focus toward your goals and maintaining boundaries, you will be years ahead of where you would be otherwise.

CHAPTER 5
Puzzle-Piece Strengths

Have you had someone tell you to use your strengths, and you immediately question what you're even good at?

We're taught from a very young age that we should invest in our weaknesses before our strengths. If we're bad at math, we should study harder. If we're weak at writing, it's probably because we don't have enough experience. Here, we're going to celebrate our strengths before focusing on our weaknesses.

Your strengths are more important than you realize, like Scooby snacks for your career—motivating you and blasting your career into orbit. How do you discover and apply your strengths in a way that makes you stand out?

I played on a recreational basketball team a couple years ago. My friend Ben was our designated team coach. He'd bring the roster, game plan, and motivation to each game.

"Alright guys," he'd start off each game, "we got this."

I joked with Ben that he was one of the best coaches I'd ever had, and he replied that he enjoyed coaching such a good group. He liked being able to motivate us and strategize to get the win. Coaching was one of Ben's biggest strengths—both on the court and in business. He coached our basketball team, and he created a similar dynamic with his sales team.

Sometimes we have strengths in one area of our lives that we can apply to our professional world. Much like Ben was our team's basketball coach, he applied his strength to motivate, teach, and develop his professional team.

We usually think of strengths as skills that require development and training, but our strengths often start small as things we inherently do well without trying. They come so easily to us that it's as automatic as breathing, and we don't think anything of it because we assume everyone has the same experience.

Think about what you're good at and what you get excited to do.

For me, I have always been very good at puzzles. I get butterflies just thinking about Risk (the world domination strategy game). I love being able to think three turns ahead and predict the behaviors of the other players. I get excited by being intellectually challenged to constantly shift perspectives and strategies.

When I began working professionally, I assumed everyone had this strength of shifting perspectives and solving puzzles. Turns out, most people didn't. I got so frustrated when I would see a clear problem and solution that I would have to explain to my team.

"It's really not that hard," I would say to myself. "My role on this team is so easy for me because it's my strength." And, when I got to apply my strengths, I got that butterfly feeling. It felt good to be good at what I was doing.

To put it another way, you are a piece in the grand puzzle that is life. You're like the type of jigsaw puzzle that has oddly shaped interlocking pieces, and your fit in that jigsaw depends on what strengths and talents you can offer.

What interlocking pieces do you have to offer that others are looking for? For every jagged-edged strength you have, there is a puzzle looking for your fit.

My puzzle-piece strengths fit perfectly in some areas, but not in others. I find teams and projects where my interlocking edges complement the team's edges. So, the question for me became, "What other strengths can I bring to my projects and team?" In order to be more effective, I had to be extremely self-aware in where I could contribute my talents.

Typically, you would uncover your strengths through tangible work experience over a period of years, but we can do some inventories, assessments, and exercises to get a jump on that process.

Get Feedback

The most authentic (and quickest) way to learn your strengths is to ask those around you. People you work with every day sometimes know you better than you know yourself.

Seeking strength feedback from coworkers, family, and friends is something that can be enlightening if done with the right intention. The strategy here is super simple: Ask people what they've seen you do well. When you reach out, the ask doesn't have to be complicated.

I recently did this with my coworkers and friends, as shown in the following table. I sent them this quick text:

Can you help me? I'm exploring my strengths, and I'm curious about your opinion of what I do well.

Feedback from	Strengths Identified
Ann Marie (mentor)	• Can <u>build</u> a team. • <u>Visionary</u> and idea guy • <u>Empathetic</u> • Sense of <u>humor</u> • <u>Organized</u>
Kate (friend and creative partner on many projects)	• Great at <u>conceptualizing</u> the big picture • You have grand ideas and think about the aspects on <u>how they work together</u>. • Good at <u>facilitating</u> • Great <u>public speaker</u>. You know how to empathize with people up front.

Lori (friend and coworker)	• <u>Delegation</u>. You were good at showing me how to do things. • <u>Teamwork</u>. Willing to sit down and brainstorm/talk through things • <u>Networking</u>. You have an empathetic vibe that makes it easier for people to talk to you.
Abby (friend and coworker)	• <u>Pushing people</u> to their fullest potential • Making everyone <u>feel validated</u> • <u>Bringing positives</u> out in every situation
Chelsey (friend)	• You're very <u>witty.</u> • Always a <u>self-starter</u> • Definitely a <u>people person</u>

Once I got that feedback, I noticed the commonalities.

After receiving feedback about your strengths, you will start noticing some commonalities—both hard skills and soft skills.

I put my strengths into a table and underlined key points. Based on feedback from my peers, friends, and mentor, I have identified the following strengths:

- **Empathetic**—relating and engaging with others

- **Strategic**—conceptualizing and interworking
- **Teamwork**—facilitating, networking, and delegating
- **Positive**—validating and being optimistic
- **Entrepreneurial**—a self-starter and a visionary

Our strengths will evolve and grow, but this method is a great start to identifying your strengths quickly. As you think about growing them, some will give you butterflies, and some won't. For now, just focus on collecting and condensing them.

Some rules to follow with this approach:

1. Be open to any piece of feedback. While doing this exercise, you may receive feedback that you disagree with. Maybe it's negative or unconstructive. I would advise that you stay open and not become defensive. I suggest that you first seek more information from the individual who gave you the feedback. Ask if they can share more details about that particular trait. If you're still stuck on it, ask others around you if they have noticed that trait in you. And, if you've now uncovered a new weakness, bring that with you to the next chapter of this book.

2. Select the right people. You'll want to ask people who actively support you, but you may get more genuine feedback from acquaintances. Typically, acquaintances view you with less emotion, so they can give you an objective assessment.

3. Be clear on your ask. You're looking for professional development support. When you reach out, ask for

feedback on your strengths that might benefit your career and/or professional development.

Try Formal Assessments

Another way to find your strengths is by participating in some formal assessments specifically designed to help professionals. Some of these tests assess your soft skills, while others assess your ability to problem-solve or your working style. When combined, they give you a good starting point to look at your strengths through the lens of psychology and research.

If you're currently employed, some companies will pay for you to take a couple of these tests. I once managed a team that I required to take CliftonStrengths, and our company paid for the tests. It was invaluable seeing our team's gaps and strengths holistically.

Some other popular tests are the Myers-Briggs personality inventory and the DiSC profile. I can speak personally on a few tests that I have taken and would recommend.

It's important for me to note that these are just tests. They are not designed to lock you into a box or define you. Instead, they're meant to present a unique lens in which you can assess yourself. If the assessments returned don't resonate with you, you can challenge them.

Personality Assessments

Personality assessments are important because they

give insight into how you process information, your preferred methods of communication/interaction, and recommendations for how you can better work with others. Some examples are:

- Myers-Briggs (paid)—My personal favorite, this assessment indicates differing psychological preferences in how people perceive the world and make decisions. https://www.myersbriggs.org/my-mbti-personality-type/mbti-basics/home.htm?bhcp=1

- DiSC (paid)—This behavior-assessment tool is based on the DiSC theory of psychologist William Moulton Marston, which centers on four different personality traits: dominance, influence, steadiness, and conscientiousness. https://www.discprofile.com/

- 16PF (free)—This 16 Personality Factor Questionnaire is a self-report personality test developed over several decades of empirical research by Raymond B. Cattell, Maurice Tatsuoka, and Herbert Eber. https://openpsychometrics.org/tests/16PF.php

- Eysenck Personality Inventory (free)—This assessment measures two pervasive independent dimensions of personality, extraversion-introversion and neuroticism-stability, which account for most of the variance in the personality domain. http://www.iluguru.ee/test/eysencks-personality-inventory-epi-extroversionintroversion/

Professional Assessments

Professional assessments are helpful because they focus clearly on the professional workplace. Many assessments will focus on different areas—such as cultural, interpersonal, and social—that you can measure yourself against. Examples include:

- CliftonStrength (paid)—My personal favorite out of the professional strength assessments, it uncovers your natural talents within 34 themes and identifies your top five. https://www.gallupstrengthscenter.com/

- EQ-i 2.0 (paid)—The emotional quotient inventory (EQ-i 2.0) is an assessment tool used for determining your emotional and social intelligence and understanding the emotional competencies of an individual. https://www.eitrainingcompany.com/eq-i/

- Institute of Health and Human Potential (free)—IHHP helps organizations leverage the science of emotional intelligence. https://www.ihhp.com/free-eq-quiz/

- VIA Survey (free)—The VIA Survey, formerly known as the Values in Action Inventory, is a personality test that measures an individual's 24-character strengths. https://www.viacharacter.org/

These assessments and tests are good tools for measuring yourself. They're not prescriptive, but based on what you get in return, you'll be able to feel if they fit you or not.

For example, my CliftonStrengths came back as 1) Winning Others Over (WOO), 2) Strategic, 3) Positive, 4) Command, and 5) Activator. My initial reaction was that 1–3 were 100% accurate, while 4 and 5 were not. After reflecting on the results, I embraced 4 and 5 as part of my key strengths. In fact, they're major contributors to how I work with people most effectively.

I have had team members who strongly disagree with their results. In that case, I would advocate taking the test again in a month or two.

These tests are starting points for your strength-finding journey. The real goal with assessments is to find more data points that you can incorporate into your overall professional identity. If you compare the CliftonStrengths to the list I compiled from my friends, the strengths are similar.

Review Your Performance

The next step to take on your self-evaluation journey is to create a strengths inventory. You'll look at your experience and your work to come up with your inventory. Although you may be tempted to skip over this step, I recommend completing it. You can design the inventory however you want; you can create a mental list or write it down somewhere. It can be as formal as you want to make it.

Or you can create something as simple as a bullet list, like the one I did:

- Socially conscious and aware of others' needs
- Loves applying research and best practices
- Good at connecting people and ideas
- Strong communicator over various mediums/platforms

Once you create your strengths list, you can compare it against the other assessments you've done. Some items may line up, and some items may be opposites.

Comparing how others view you with your self-view will help you get aligned and make improvements toward who you want to be—and where you fit into the grand puzzle. Also, you can compare your strengths and skills with the desired skills of your industry and see where you fall.

For example, my function is marketing. The top soft skills for marketers include leadership, adaptability, and collaboration—all of which are part of my self-inventory.

Although my example seems clear-cut, sometimes there's a disconnect. You may notice your strengths don't fit your industry or function as cleanly. In that case, you have some unique options. You can search for an industry that is a better fit, become a change agent and innovator in your space, or grow your industry-relevant strengths.

As you strive to create an exciting career, you can strategically use your strengths to build and sustain one. The first step is always to explore your strengths. The next step is to build on those muscles and flex your strengths. Your strengths make you a unique puzzle piece, and by owning them, you'll find plenty of places where you fit into the jigsaw puzzle that is life.

CHAPTER 6
What's Your Hot Button?

Weaknesses often come with internal shame, a sense of inadequacy. Then those weaknesses turn into *hot buttons* that can cause you to be embarrassed when they're exposed. And then you may feel compelled to fix your weaknesses to avoid that embarrassment. Weaknesses can be a big shame—but you can find ways to ensure they won't control you.

Before you get sucked into that shame spiral, let's take a step back. What are weaknesses really? Weaknesses are not defined as "things I'm bad at." They are skills that take more effort to perfect than you think should be required.

For example, I have tried to learn accounting, but I just cannot get it. I've spent hours and hours trying to learn, and I come up with nothing.

As a natural rule for most professionals, tasks that allow you to use your strengths give you butterflies and fulfillment. On the other hand, projects that force you to improve your weaknesses drain your energy and overall excitement—like my attempt to learn accounting. In order to be truly excited by your work, you need to know how to manage your weaknesses—which to improve and which to ignore.

Let's get into it:

- What are your weaknesses?
- Which weaknesses should you improve?
- What strengths can you pull from to compensate for your weaknesses?
- How do you manage weaknesses in a team setting?

A great children's book called *Giraffes Can't Dance*, by Giles Andreae and Guy Parker-Rees, illustrates an appropriate lesson. Each year in this fictional jungle, all the animals attend an event called the Jungle Dance. Every species has a unique dance they perform that caters to their body style, stamina, and personality. Gerald, a giraffe, is incapable of doing any of these dances because of his long, awkward legs, hence the title, *Giraffes Can't Dance*. He tries mimicking the other animals' dances and fails.

Eventually Gerald comes to realize that he's born to dance a different dance. He uses his awkward legs and long neck to create a dance unlike any that has existed before. The other animals applaud, and we all the learn the *critically important* lesson of being ourselves.

Professionally speaking, we're all awkward giraffes who need to embrace our own dance. We see other people's strengths, and we assume that we need to have the same strengths in order to succeed. We should instead challenge the notion that we need to fix all our imperfections in order to succeed; investing in our strengths is a far better use of our time.

All great business leaders are known for their strengths. Almost all of them use their strengths to counteract their weaknesses. Steve Jobs, for example, was a design and innovation genius known for bringing elegance and sophistication to technology. He was also an extreme micromanager and lacked empathy. In most leaders, these would be detrimental flaws.

Jobs used his strengths in design, innovation, elegance, and ideation to counterbalance his weaknesses. Now, imagine if he had focused less on design and innovation and had instead focused on empathy. Would we have the iPhone?

Oprah Winfrey, another great leader, is known for her empathy, compassion, and ability to build relationships. She's created a career by connecting with others and helping people understand very sensitive and complex ideas. Winfrey admits in an *Oprah's The Life You Want Weekend* speech that her two biggest weaknesses are that she can't let things go easily and she avoids confrontation.[7]

Like Jobs, Winfrey is known for her strengths, not her weaknesses. Imagine a world where Winfrey had focused on conflict resolution instead of empathy. We'd have a very different world.

The point is that you may have weaknesses, but your

---

7   Oprah Winfrey, "Oprah's 2 Greatest Weaknesses," October 28, 2014, video, 1:25, http://www.oprah.com/oprahstour/oprah-shares-her-2-greatest-weaknesses-video_1.

strengths will define you, so focus on them. You do need to know your weaknesses, however, so that you can mitigate the risk associated with them.

Knowing and managing your weaknesses are critical steps in your path to development. Knowing your weaknesses will allow you to better lead teams and develop a plan to pull on your strengths.

Identifying and Managing Your Personal Weaknesses

We each have an individual obligation to self-awareness. In your process of self-awareness, you'll need to separate your weaknesses into two categories: areas for improvement and skills-based weaknesses.

AREAS OF IMPROVEMENT

While many weaknesses can be ignored, you will have some areas for improvement that you will want to address. Identifying these early and working on them allows you to move forward with a well-rounded professional approach. Areas of improvement are typically major skills you need to improve to move forward and that would otherwise hold you back. These are skills that are necessary for your job, and these are the two types of areas for improvement that you will need to consider: mission-critical skills and hot-button triggers.

If you are drawn to be a teacher but are a poor public speaker, for example, that is a mission-critical area for improvement that you need to execute your job. These types of areas for improvement are fluid depending on your position. All organizations have required skills for every position, so be prepared to learn new skills with every position you take. If you're looking for skills to improve within your role, a good starting point would be doing some research to find the hard and soft skills typically required for your job.

An example of this in practice is a leader like King George VI, sovereign of the United Kingdom in the early 20th century. King George VI had a speech impediment that prevented him from communicating effectively with his kingdom. As portrayed in the movie The King's Speech, he saw his speech as an area of improvement and felt it was mission critical to his leadership, especially in the golden era of radio.

While King George VI could've focused only on his strengths, he felt that his ability to communicate clearly was mission critical. (As he was the leader of a nation, I would agree.) So, he worked to improve it.

Your other area for improvement in your job is your hot-button trigger. Your triggers include skills or situations that give you a negative emotional response and can prevent you from being professional. Everyone has them, and they usually don't go away easily.

For example, you may have anxiety that is deep seated. If you get anxious when you're put in stressful situations, you may want to work through that hot-button trigger so that it doesn't affect your job. Your triggers are typically harder to uncover than the mission-critical skills above, but if you ignore them, they may manifest as negative outcomes in your job without your knowing.

SKILLS-BASED WEAKNESSES

The second major category of personal weakness includes your skills-based weaknesses. These are skills that are not required for your career and are more general in nature. These weaknesses are typically things you could ignore and not focus effort on.

In general, however, it is smart to know your skills-based weaknesses so that you don't get caught flat-footed as you progress in your career. That is to say, you should always know your weaknesses so that they don't hinder your advancement.

An example of a skills-based weakness might be that you are not good at kick-starting or instigating new projects. Whenever you try and develop a new plan, you struggle with developing the overall scope, assembling a team, and creating an action plan. In this situation, and with your different skill set, you may not need to learn how to instigate projects.

Not everyone is born as an "Activator" or "Command" (to borrow from CliftonStrengths), and that's okay. Knowing that your skill set lies more in the details than the instigation will allow you to position yourself as the foundation that your projects can stand on.

Then, as you move up in leadership—assuming that's what you want to do—you can build a team around you that covers your weak areas.

Identifying and Managing Team Weaknesses

Mitigating your weaknesses is a lot easier when you're working on a team. Typically, the best teams function when team members are dependent on each other in a sort of symbiotic relationship. Whether you are leading a team or contributing to a team, you are obligated to share your weaknesses and align your strengths. A great team leader can identify team weaknesses and align team strengths to complete projects effectively.

I once managed a small (but powerful) team of marketers. My team was heavily focused on marketing strategy and various team members had strengths in operation, communication, customer experience, digital, and content. And, everyone was generally empathic and socially invested in the other team members.

However, we lacked a sense of "relationship building." We didn't naturally have strong relationship bonds as other teams had. As the leader of that team, I had to put in effort to build relationships across the team. I learned that one of my team members was a strong relationship builder—that was her natural strength.

I approached this team member to ask for her help. She was more than happy to use her strengths in a creative way. Since then, the teamwork has become even stronger, and team members feel more comfortable bringing ideas and contributions to a wider range of projects.

Unfortunately, not every team is as perfectly balanced as my team was.

When you work on teams, the weakness rule still applies—focus on your strengths and mitigate your weaknesses. Team leaders can help their teams find the butterflies in their work, and typically those teams function a lot more productively when they pull on their strengths.

Weaknesses can be uncomfortable to talk about, but acknowledging and owning them are the first steps in finding more meaningful work. Finding work that makes you excited and gives you butterflies doesn't happen by accident. You need to make a conscious choice in where to invest your time.

And remember: Not every weakness needs to be fixed.

CHAPTER 7
Canada: The 51st State

When you start working, you want everything to happen at once. You want responsibility, to lead projects, and to be engaged with the team. You want to make an immediate impact. And even though you've experienced only a small amount, you're confident that you know enough.

Let me warn you: You don't. When you join a new company, you need a little more experience in order to make the right moves. So, why do we get overly confident about things we know nothing about?

After I graduated from college, I had an amazing job waiting for me in New York City with an international media company. I walked in my first day well-equipped with the knowledge I would need to succeed. I excitedly received my responsibilities and began working.

I felt like I was on top of the world. New job. New city. New friends. Energized with new ideas, I started pitching recommended changes that would impact our department, my workload, and the company. Some of them stuck, but a lot of them were dismissed.

"How irritating," I thought to myself. Obviously, my recommended changes were well-founded and based on my *limited* experience at the company. But what I didn't realize is that I really didn't know anything—even though I thought I did.

The Dunning-Kruger Effect

The Dunning-Kruger Effect is a cognitive bias where people with little knowledge of a topic overestimate themselves, while more intelligent people underestimate their knowledge.

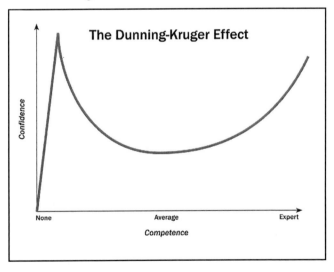

Figure from PsychologyToday.com[8]

---

[8] William Poundstone, "The Dunning-Kruger President," *Psychology Today*, January 21, 2017, https://www.psychologytoday.com/us/blog/head-in-the-cloud/201701/the-dunning-kruger-president.

CANADA: THE 51ST STATE

When presented with a new situation or knowledge, we typically start with a very high sense of confidence, even when our knowledge is low. The more knowledge we begin to acquire on a topic, the lower our confidence goes until we truly learn the nuances of that topic, industry, or function.

Typically, this effect presents itself in times of information overload. Our brains can't process how to decipher the information, so it follows previous shortcuts or "beliefs" that existed before.

That's a complicated way of saying that when people are unsure, their brains trick them into being sure.

Jimmy Kimmel does a segment on his TV show Jimmy Kimmel Live called "Lie Witness News" that demonstrates Dunning-Kruger in action.[9] He will find pedestrians on the street and ask them their opinion on a made-up event.

On one segment, Jimmy's producer asked pedestrians how they feel about Canada becoming America's 51st state. Obviously, that didn't happen because Canada is still its own country:

> *Interviewer:* How did you react to the news that Canada is becoming America's 51st state?
>
> *Informed Pedestrian:* I was shocked, honestly. Out of all the countries they could incorporate, I'm surprised they chose Canada.

It's funny and terrifying. We laugh so we don't cry. But,

---

9 Jimmy Kimmel, "Lie Witness News – Canada Is America's 51st State," June 13, 2019, video, 3:13, https://www.youtube.com/watch?v=ReN82pdVZ4c.

professionally speaking, we all have terrifyingly stupid responses to things we know nothing about. The less we know, the more overconfidence we have.

For example, I started my career as a content creator for our company. I ran our social channels (Facebook, Twitter, Instagram, and LinkedIn). I had used these platforms in a personal capacity, but I hadn't yet done business marketing through them.

"No worries," I thought to myself, "social media is super easy." I quickly learned that it's not easy at all. Entire companies are dedicated to social media marketing, and my three months of experience could not compete—no matter how confident I was.

That's the Dunning-Kruger Effect in practice.

As a professional, you'll need to understand that even though you feel confident about a topic, you more than likely don't have enough knowledge to make the impact you want (yet). If you want to make a long-lasting impact on your companies and the world, you'll need more knowledge and experience. The fastest way to get that knowledge is through experience.

70-20-10 Learning Model

So, you're overconfident, and you need more knowledge. What's the fastest way to learn?

Your first gut instinct might be to depend on your company's talent development department to create your learning path and map out your continued learning. Unfortunately, many of you won't be able to rely on your companies to develop you at the rate that you're craving, so you'll need to develop yourself.

When building out your continuing development plan, try using the 70-20-10 model.

In this model, you'll dedicate 70 percent of your time to experiential learning, such as new projects and experiences. You'll dedicate 20 percent of your time to social learning, such as receiving advice from mentors or coaches. And you'll dedicate 10 percent of your time to formal learning, such classes and training programs.

Typically, when you begin looking at your career growth, you'll limit yourself to current positions. For example, if you're a sales associate, you may build your career growth in hopes of someday becoming Vice President of Sales—a position that may or may not exist at your company in 10 years. As you follow predestined paths for careers that continuously evolve due to business trends, technology, and the pace of innovation, companies are hiring more and more for potential instead of existing experience.

EXPERIENTIAL: 70 PERCENT
To learn through experience, you start by acknowledging that all projects have lessons to be learned—no matter how small the task.

What are the primary projects you currently work on? Some projects may be below your skill set. A bulk of your work projects should be in your comfort zone (or slightly above). And you should have a set of projects that are stretches for you—projects you feel underqualified for. If you don't have stretch projects, find some. If you envision a long-term future at your current company, be sure to network with your supervisor and cross-company leaders to find stretch projects. Try and get exposure to as many departments as you can.

What learnings are you pulling out of your current projects? Sometimes these are small lessons like "I learned a new feature on a software," or they can be big like "I realize I don't want to do this the rest of my life." Either way, look for lessons. And, if you can, try and make them positive. If you begin focusing on positive lessons, you'll typically have a better employment experience overall because you will program your brain to seek confirmation bias.

Where do you want to go? It's important to envision your career path. You won't be able to know where you'll be 10 or more years from now, but you can plan where you want to be one or two years from now. Your 10-year goal will fill in once you get some momentum behind you.

Get yourself going, and you'll start to notice trends. Make sure to pay attention to the butterflies. Usually, if you cannot articulate where you want to go in the next couple years, your butterflies will give you emotional direction to support you in your development.

SOCIAL: 20 PERCENT
Social learning comes from your connections, network,

or mentors. Be open to these lessons because they can come in any form—directly, through observations, via storytelling, etc. These lessons can be professionally oriented, but more valuably, these lessons can be personal.

One of my mentors/friends will always be available to advise me professionally. And, she knows me so well that I can ask for personal advice that will improve my work. For example, I was struggling with my supervisor. My supervisor and I had had several miscommunications that had led to tension and a strained relationship. I reached out to my mentor to seek advice, and she rightfully said that I needed to make personal adjustments before moving forward.

That level of personalized advice and learning is critically important. Surrounding yourself with supportive and well-meaning people will set you up for social-learning success. And from that handful of three or four people, be comfortable and open to receiving their feedback.

FORMAL: 10 PERCENT

Formal learning is the smallest percent of the 70-20-10 learning framework. You'll seek formal learning when you want to sharpen specific skills.

You should constantly be learning and improving, and as a young professional, it's important to acknowledge that you have a lot more learning to do. Your need or want to make an impact never really goes away; it just becomes more realistic.

If your need to make an impact is strong, redirect

that passion to learning instead of telling other people how you think they should operate. Controlling your overconfidence and focusing on learning will put you years ahead of your peers. And, at some point, you will know enough to make that impact. There's not really a sign that tells you when you're ready; it's more of a feeling.

If you go from feeling extremely confident about a topic to realizing you know nothing, that's usually a positive indicator that you're turning a corner. When you start to say, "it's complicated," you're probably at a point where you can make an impact.

You may not know enough to make the impact you want right now, and that's okay.

CHAPTER 8
No Cell Phones at the Dinner Table

Put your phone down—this is important.

There's pressure in the workforce to be technologically competent, to "get with the times." But that connection often goes too far.

The next critical step in growing your career is mastering your use of technology without letting it own you. This includes knowing the value of your attention, finding the proper work-life balance, and breaking bad tech habits that are holding you back.

The Attention Economy

In our lifetimes, we've seen a remarkable shift in the fundamentals of our economy. Our ability to positively navigate that change gives us a strong competitive advantage.

From the 1970s until the early 2000s, our economy

thrived on the service industry. In more recent years, that service economy has shifted to the attention economy. We're living in a time where the most valuable commodity is our "eyeballs."

It's a nasty cycle. We are the product that tech companies are selling to advertisers, who are then selling to us. And many of us don't understand the lasting impact of this cycle on our personal and professional lives. As technology integrates better into our lives, we need to understand how to use it more powerfully to amplify our success without falling victim to the pitfalls.

I got a new iPhone recently, and I noticed it had a feature to track and limit my usage. Interested in running an experiment, I turned on my tracking and told my iPhone to lock social media apps after a couple hours of usage.

The first day, I made it to lunch before I went through my allotted social media time. The next day, I made it to 11 a.m. At the end of that week, I got a report from Apple: "Your average iPhone use this week was 5 hours and 10 minutes per day." For those doing the math at home, that's more than 36 hours a week that I spent on my phone.

We waste so much time doing nothing. According to a Nielsen study, in the first quarter of 2018, adults in the U.S. spent more than 11 hours a day in front of a screen—TV, computer, tablet, phone, game console, etc.[10]

---

10   Quentin Fottrell, "People Spend Most of Their Waking Hours Staring at Screens," *MarketWatch*, August 14, 2018, https://www.marketwatch.com/story/people-are-spending-most-of-their-waking-hours-staring-at-screens-2018-08-01.

Based on Nielsen's research, those numbers continue to climb year over year. We spend a significant amount of the time outside of work being attached to our screens. Every hour we're on a screen, someone is making money—and it's most likely not us.

It's time we take back our attention and invest it where it benefits us.

Taking Back Your Attention

We all have 24 hours in a day. So, we naturally ask, "How do the most successful people allocate their 24 hours?"

Harvard Business Review ran a survey to study how top-performing CEOs spend their time.[11]

- 56% of time spent meeting with others
- 26% of time spent alone on individual/independent tasks
- 10% of time spent on personal matters
- 8% of time spent traveling

The CEOs in HBR's survey had one thing in common: They were strategic about where they invested their time; nothing was taken for granted.

The quick lesson: You need to cut the "fat" on wasted or misused time because your attention is valuable. A lot

---

11 Oriana Bandiera, Stephen Hansen, Andrea Prat, and Raffaella Sadun, "A Survey of How 1,000 CEOs Spend Their Day Reveals What Makes Leaders Successful," Harvard Business Review, October 12, 2017, https://hbr.org/2017/10/a-survey-of-how-1000-ceos-spend-their-day-reveals-what-makes-leaders-successful.

of times, you can cut time from your technology use and get immediate results.

HOW CAN YOU BETTER USE TECHNOLOGY TO MAKE YOUR TIME MORE PRODUCTIVE?

Technology generally allows you to do more with less—in theory. If you're looking to expand your personal capability with technology, make sure you're using the right technology. Investing in flashy devices or hyped apps doesn't mean you're going to be more effective. It helps to start in analog mode and then figure out where you can go digital.

For example, I tried downloading a bunch of task management apps, and realized that none of them really worked for me. So, I went back to analog (non-digital) notetaking. I invested in some nice Moleskine notebooks and became much more productive.

Don't try and force fit technology if it doesn't work for you. Also, take advantage of automation where you can.

When I started my career, I worked as a social media marketer. My company, at that point, hadn't invested in automation tools for my role. After months of creating and posting data manually, I searched for alternative methods of scheduling, aggregating, and measuring success. The small technology investment allowed me to gain more time back for other activities.

HOW DO YOU USE TECHNOLOGY TO STAY INFORMED?

Technology is great for connecting you with information—

sometimes almost too effectively. When it comes to news about your profession, industry, or business, news sources are usually reliable. Media outlets such as Bloomberg, Harvard Business Review, and Forbes offer valuable business news and strategies.

If you use technology to stay informed, be critical about where that information is coming from and the biases attached. According to Pew Research Center, 95 percent of Americans get their news on some sort of screen—TV or online..[12] And, for those between 18 and 29, 50 percent of their news gathering happens solely online. Of those finding information online, 86 percent admit being "duped" by fake news, according to a global study by the Centre for International Governance Innovation (CIGI).[13]

Your attention is valuable. If you're directing your attention toward information gathering, find a reliable source and be critical of the information. If it sounds off, it probably is.

HOW CAN YOU USE TECHNOLOGY TO RELAX?

During normal work hours, you should take breaks every hour or so. And, you might assume that a good distraction would be checking your social media or texting your mom. Did you know that the average American spends

---

[12] Amy Mitchell, Jeffrey Gottfried, Michael Barthel, and Elisa Shearer, "1. Pathways to News," Pew Research Center, July 7, 2016, https://www.journalism.org/2016/07/07/pathways-to-news/.,

[13] Phys.org, "86 Percent of Internet Users Admit Being Duped by Fake News: Survey," June 12, 2019, https://phys.org/news/2019-06-percent-internet-users-duped-fake.html.

six to nine hours a day on digital devices.[14]

If you're going to use technology to relax, try some techniques that don't require staring at a screen. Maybe turn on your favorite Spotify playlist and take a walk. Or listen to an audio book. Better yet, shut down your tech for a couple minutes and meditate.

When it comes to tech, feeling relaxed isn't the same as being distracted.

How do you achieve work-life balance with constant contact?

It's vital to set boundaries for when, where, and how you allow "work" and "life" to mix—in hopes of finding the right work-life balance.

With technology constantly connecting you, work is often only a couple clicks away. The trick with work-life integration is that it's something you create. Balancing work and life will have to be a conscious effort.

When working to create work-life integration, do so with your time as well as with your social media channels. Make sure to check your employer's rules for social media.

According to Pew Research Center, 29 percent of workers (18–29 years old) have discovered information via social media that has lowered their opinion of a

---

14 Jory MacKay, "7 Science-Backed Ways to Take Better Breaks," Zapier, September 25, 2017, https://zapier.com/blog/better-breaks/.
03/22

colleague.[15]

Regardless of whether you're on or off the clock, you're a representative of the company, and the content you post online might not be deemed appropriate by your employers.

Breaking Bad Technology Habits

If you're serious about owning your attention again, you'll need to break your old technology-use habits. Books like The Power of Habit by Charles Duhigg are good places to start to get a deeper dive on breaking habits. For the sake of time, I will give you the quick tutorial.

According to Psychology Today, breaking bad habits isn't about stopping. Psychologically speaking, we can't "break" habits; we simply adopt new ones. We find substitutes.[16] Here's a quick six steps I've adapted from Psychology Today to get you started on breaking those bad technology habits and back to owning your attention.

---

15 Cliff Lampe and Nicole B. Ellison, "Social Media and the Workplace," Pew Research Center, June 22, 2016, https://www.pewinternet.org/2016/06/22/social-media-and-the-workplace/.

16 Robert Taibbi, L.C.S.W., "How to Break Bad Habits," Psychology Today, December 15, 2017, https://www.psychologytoday.com/us/blog/fixing-families/201712/how-break-bad-habits.

STEP ONE: IDENTIFY THE BEHAVIOR YOU WANT TO CHANGE

First, you'll need to identify the behavior you want to change. As it relates to technology, it could be something as basic as "I want to be more mindful about my technology use" or it could be more specific, such as the need to change your social media behavior and lower your overall social media use.

STEP TWO: IDENTIFY AND CHALLENGE THE TRIGGER

This might get tricky. What currently drives your current behavior? Once you know that, you can catch yourself once it happens. For me, whenever I got bored, I would automatically open my apps. It got to the point where I would sometimes not even remember opening my phone, but somehow, I was in the app. Eventually, I started catching myself "getting bored" and would ask myself what other things I could do besides open my phone.

STEP THREE: DEVELOP A SUBSTITUTE PLAN

You can't really "break" a bad habit. You'll need to redirect it to something else or substitute something else for it. So, once you catch yourself, what are you going to do instead?

This was easy for me. When I got bored and caught myself, I actively chose to take a walk around the office and bother coworkers.

STEP FOUR: CHANGE THE LARGER PATTERN

Every bad habit has a larger associated pattern. If you think of your behavior as the symptom, what is the main cause?

In my case, my larger pattern was bored-ness. Why was I constantly bored at work and how could I find better use of my time? The problem I was facing wasn't that I was using social media too much; it was that I wasn't engaged with better projects.

In order to change that, I talked with my supervisor about creating more meaningful work. After that point, I didn't need social media to fill the time, because I was more excited about doing other things.

STEP FIVE: USE PROMPTS

Prompts are signs or "memos" you can create to remind yourself of the behavior you want to change. Think sticky notes.

For example, since all my social media apps were in one spot, I moved the app locations on my phone. Then, every time I wanted to check social media (out of habit), my apps wouldn't be there. That prompt reminded me to use social media intentionally.

STEP SIX: SUPPORT AND REWARD YOURSELF

Last but not least, give yourself a prize when you gain some momentum.

At the end of the week, I would treat myself to a cherry Coke if I kept my social media levels down. Now I have a soda addiction, but that's a topic for another book...

Once you master your use of technology, you'll give yourself more space to breathe and think. And, if all goes according to plan, you'll stop distracting yourself from feeling your butterflies when they do start fluttering.

CHAPTER 9
The Diamond Effect

You're going to face adversity throughout your career—including people trying to keep you from succeeding. Here's what you'll need in order to face those people.

Let's start by defining adversity, according to Merriam-Webster.

Adversity (noun): a state or instance of serious or continued difficulty or misfortune.

The general perception of adversity is that it's something happening to us, and I don't know if that's completely true. In my mind, you can experience two types of adversity: toxic adversity and healthy adversity. And you can learn from both.

Toxic adversity is a struggle aimed at tearing you down on a personal level. Some examples are ageism, sexism, or racism. Although we wish toxic adversity didn't exist in the workplace, it absolutely does. In a professional environment, toxic adversity is usually personal and designed to hinder your growth.

Healthy adversity, which is far more common, is the struggle that challenges you to grow and develop professionally. These are challenges or setbacks that force you to work harder or shift your perspective to accomplish your goal. Examples might include a stretch project, role reassignment, or difficult client.

You will generally encounter more struggle as you become more successful. If you become successful in your organization or on your team, you'll often face more toxic and healthy adversity. When you experience adversity, it may be tempting to stop trying and become complacent. You can manage adversity several ways, but throwing in the towel shouldn't be your first choice.

When I was 23, I found myself at an amazing company with many more responsibilities than I could handle. Due to some employee turnover and reorganization, I reported directly to the CEO of an 800-million-dollar–plus organization. At first, I was tempted to shy away from my new responsibilities and stick to the status quo. But, recognizing the potential, I pushed forward.

One of my responsibilities was organizing and planning our company's sponsorship presence at an international festival in Cannes, France. My budget was just under $2 million.

Had I ever managed a budget that large? Nope.

Had I ever been to Europe? Unfortunately, no.

Did I have experience running sponsorships? Ha. Sure didn't.

Over the next couple months, I took on the task of planning this massive event. I managed air travel and hotels for 12 VIP executives, planned several high-profile client dinners, booked two speaking engagements featuring internationally recognized talent, and advertised our activities.

The intense pressure I felt from this event challenged my skills like I'd never experienced before. I thought I was going to explode. In the end, it all went swimmingly. I received positive feedback from clients, executives, and colleagues. It was a win for the record books.

This event was an example of healthy adversity for me. While it was painful in the moment, I gained many valuable skills and applicable knowledge. And, most importantly, I learned that making diamonds is an intense process.

The Diamond Effect

For diamonds to be made, the conditions need to be perfect. They start off as random carbon molecules deep in the earth's mantle. Then, intense amounts of heat and pressure are applied. After thousands of years, the basic elements begin to crystalize and re-form into raw diamond.

Diamonds withstand incredible force, and that pressure creates some of the strongest material in the world. The physical adversity creates one tough rock.

Metaphorically speaking, we are all diamonds in the making.

Early in our careers, we're nothing but potential. We enter the workforce ready to be molded by experience. The pressure and adversity we feel at work supply the force we need to become a diamond.

In my experience, I have reached very clear points of "fight or flight" when I could either stick out the adversity, or I could fold like a poorly made house of cards.

Adversity can scare us. The difference between the average and the awesome is that people who embrace (healthy) adversity come out stronger and more valuable.

That's the diamond effect in action.

Managing Adversity

Sometimes being confronted with adversity is tough, and although you want to grow, you may not know how to manage the struggle.

In the case of toxic adversity, your solution will be a personal one, so consult with trusted mentors, advisors, and friends for help and support. Many organizations have formal avenues to address toxic adversity, and in the worst cases, help can come from outside the company.

Seeking help from inside or outside your organization may seem scary, but you're likely to find a community and resources that will help you through those difficult challenges. Everyone has a right to be respected, and you shouldn't feel uncomfortable being yourself.

In the case of healthy adversity, you can use the six following strategies to help you stay resilient in a time of adversity.

1. Shift Your Perspective

The first strategy is to shift your perspective of the situation. Sometimes when you engage with a situation, you perceive it as impossible when it's completely possible.

Instead, you could rethink a situation to make it easier to manage. Take that impossible project off your unrealistic pedestal and bring it down to earth.

In my Cannes example, I approached the situation stating all of the experience I didn't have. I eventually engaged with the project once I shifted my perspective and realized how qualified I really was to manage that program. My internal dialogue went from "I'm in way over my head" to, "This is right in my wheelhouse, and I look forward to the experience."

That shift from "I can't" to "I can" will help you feel like you're owning your experience.

2. Find Collaborators and Partners

Address the situation objectively and find where your unique strengths fit. Then, once you know where your gaps are, find people who can cover your weaknesses.

This is one of my favorite strategies when dealing with adversity. I love collaborating with others, and people are usually excited to share the experience.

At the age of 23, I had plenty of weaknesses that could have hindered the success of the project. By working with partners and collaborators, however, we owned the event together and made it a massive success. The Cannes team was engaging, supportive, and effective, and that experience is one that we all shared.

When you're up against a challenge, you'd be surprised at who will step up and help if you just ask.

3. Reset Yourself

Sometimes the work can be intense. Especially on extremely pressing work, you can feel depleted. You may then feel like you can't bring your full self to the project. It's time to reset yourself, whatever that looks like for you.

Sometimes it might be a quick walk outside in the fresh air. For me, it's a 10-minute meditation. My friend Chelsey loves getting a massage and a smoothie when she needs to reset.

We all have our own methods of getting calm. Test strategies and find one that works for you. (Our brains love this approach, by the way.)

You may have had a moment, for example, when you were in class and stuck on a math problem. Then you left and ate dinner, and when you went back to the problem, the solution was so clear. That's because your brain continues to work on problem solving even when you're no longer directly addressing the problem.

By directing your attention somewhere else, your brain will be able to work through the situation. When you return to the problem more refreshed, your brain might magically have the solution.

4. Develop a Decision Tree

Writing out problems on a piece of paper can help you resolve them.

For projects with endless decisions, a decision tree might be a good solution for you. Decision trees were originally developed by computer science researcher Ross Quinlan as a solution that allows you to play through multiple scenarios without deep diving into each one.[17] You start with your primary problem and branch two decisions from that. You continue developing solutions until you get to the roots.

A friend of mine was job hunting and trying to weigh his options. He asked me how to narrow down his search, given all the factors. We identified that each job would have pros and cons, but they also had requirements. See the decision tree we created below for the jobs that would be acceptable and not acceptable given his criteria.

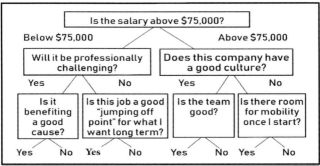

[17] JR Quinlan, "Induction of Decision Trees," *Kluwer Academic Publishers*, August 1, 1985, https://hunch.net/~coms-4771/quinlan.pdf.

In our example, he would be ok with the outcomes that result in "Go". For the results that end in "no go", he would decline the offer.

In general, decision trees help you clarify your thinking. They allow you to formally write out outcomes and help make stronger decisions.

5. Grin and Bear It
If you're still pushing through and the earlier strategies haven't worked, you might just have to suck it up and do it. This approach is a little blunt, but sometimes it's all we have. Whatever challenge you're feeling from a project, it will (hopefully) soon pass.

I once heard a great hack that helps me put things into perspective when I'm faced with the "Grin and Bear It" strategy. Think one year from where you are right now. Whatever challenge you're facing now will no longer be an issue then.

6. Find an Exit Strategy
Walking away is another option. Sometimes pushing through and being resilient isn't enough.

In cases where the work is affecting your mental and physical health, don't be afraid to walk away. In doing so, be sure to create a thought-out plan for your exit. As tempting as it might be to throw your hands up and curse people out, it's rarely the most effective exit strategy.

I once worked for a toxic supervisor who belittled my accomplishments and devalued my confidence.

After seven or eight months of trying to problem solve, I eventually had to throw in the towel and walk away. There is no shame in acknowledging that a situation isn't working.

If you do get to a point of walking away, make sure to leave as gracefully as you can. Maintain your dignity and allow the other parties to maintain theirs.

Your ability to identify and manage adversity in your professional life will pay dividends. As you strive to live an intentional life, it becomes more difficult to navigate the world without adversity.

The key is to let that adversity serve you and better you. You're a diamond in the making, and your resilience toward challenge will give you the experience and courage to succeed.

CHAPTER 10
Be Like Mike

Some people who seem to get ahead can be extremely arrogant. We have all seen these people—people like Regina George (*Mean Girls*) or Jordan Belfort (*The Wolf of Wall Street*), the conceited, egotistical bullies who run the show.

It can drive you to wonder, *Should I be more like that? Is it better to act like the prototypical assertive alpha type* (even to the point of arrogance) in order to get what you want?

The short answer is no. The longer answer is that arrogant leaders often have severe insecurities that lead them to lower others instead of elevating the team. In the short term, these individuals may appear to have success. In the long term, this type of behavior will create problems and isolate them from their end goals.

Many of us don't admire the arrogant. We're annoyed by them. The leaders we generally admire are wise, strategic, and charismatic. Unlike arrogant leaders, humble leaders are statistically proven to create high-performing teams, increase collaboration and employee engagement, and take businesses from good to great.[18]

In my early career, I started to notice that all great leaders share a superpower: humility. And although we may dismiss humility at first, it's important that we learn how to tap that skill because that's where our lasting success will emerge.

An online search for "humility" provides many different definitions. Some tell us it means to lower our self-importance, while others say that it means we're levelheaded. To cut through the clutter, I've created a definition of humility:

Humility is a confident, quiet knowing of your self-worth and the understanding that you're only human—just like everyone else.

In popular culture, humility stereotypically implies people "devaluing" themselves, but I don't believe truly humble people view themselves as worthless. Instead, they know their worth, and they don't feel compelled to have that worth validated by others.

Humility is typically thought of as a personality trait or virtue. I would argue that humility is also an interpersonal skill (superpower) much like motivation or active listening. And because it is a skill, we can learn to control and refine it to better ourselves and our careers.

---

18 Jeff Hyman, "Why Humble Leaders Make the Best Leaders," *Forbes*, October 31, 2018, https://www.forbes.com/sites/jeffhyman/2018/10/31/humility/#5bfcc0971c80.

Our best use of humility is as a lens to improve our decision making and overall attitudes—to keep us grounded and in touch with our humanity.

In 1978, a high school student tried out for his school's basketball team. The team had 15 spots and 50 kids were trying out. As a 5'10" sophomore, he wasn't a prime candidate, but he had hope.

Eager to see the tryout results, the young man sprinted to the freshly posted roster only to find he hadn't made the team. Seeing celebration and hearing laughter from his taller classmates were reminders to him that he just wasn't good enough.

Disappointed, he went home, locked the door, and started crying. With a sizeable chip on his shoulder, he got to work —determined to make the team the following year. "Whenever I was working out and got tired and figured I ought to stop, I'd close my eyes and see that list in the locker room without my name on it," the young man said.

The next year, 1979, he'd grown another four inches. His new height paired with his refined basketball skills positioned him well for the varsity team. After making the team, he quickly became a star player.

A few years later, he became a member of the University of North Carolina Tar Heels men's basketball team. Although he'd become the best player on his high school team, he remained levelheaded and confident.

The 5'10" sophomore grew and eventually reached

the NBA, where he created a dynasty—winning six championship rings and being named MVP five times. His name was Michael Jordan, one of the greatest basketball players ever. However, despite his overwhelming success, Jordan was featured in a Nike ad saying, "I have missed more than 9,000 shots in my career. I have lost almost 300 games. I have failed over and over and over again in my life. And that is why I succeed."

What a lesson in humility.

After facing rejection, Jordan worked to become the best version of himself—remaining grounded and approaching his work with a growth mentality. "I can always be better." And after winning on the court, he jumped (from the free throw line) into business. He built a successful franchise—movies, shoes, clothing, etc. Jordan's legacy lives on years after he left the court—people are still trying to "be like Mike."

HOW CAN YOU USE HUMILITY TO MAKE YOURSELF A MORE IMPACTFUL LEADER?

1. Know Where Your Worth Comes From

If you find yourself shaken by other people's opinions of you, apply your lens of humility. Be content with where you are. This might mean removing comparison from your perspective, at least in the short term.

I once saw investor Warren Buffett outside a Dairy Queen, enjoying a Blizzard. "I wonder what kind of Blizzard he got," I remember thinking. I was in high school at the time, and from then on, I set my aspirations to be a billionaire who enjoyed fast-food ice cream on Sundays.

Growing up in Omaha, I had always had a fascination with Buffett. His name was on every building, and what a powerful name it is. He could live anywhere, though, so why Omaha? Many things about Buffett's lifestyle surprised me. For example, what other billionaires would have a 6,500-square-foot house?

I've since learned that Buffett's life and worth are not determined by how big his house is, how much he spends on ice cream, or which city he lives in. The worth of a humble leader comes from within. Know you're worthy, and you'll be untouchable.

2. Understand What Feedback Is

Sometimes you'll get feedback—either solicited or unsolicited—that you don't agree with. Even when you don't agree, you can be thankful for feedback, because without it, you wouldn't have the contrast that promotes growth. Learn to process feedback via humility and see it as an opportunity.

Elizabeth Gilbert, author of Eat, Pray, Love, found overwhelming success with her first book. During a TED Talk, Gilbert admitted she was terrified to write another book after Eat, Pray, Love because she was afraid her audience wouldn't like her next book as much as the first.

During her talk, Gilbert explained that in either case—in her extreme success or her extreme failure—she was weighing others' feedback as objectively good or objectively bad. In her early experience, positive feedback meant success, and negative feedback meant failure.

That success or failure, Gilbert explained, didn't define her value as a writer. And, in fact, the labels we all associate with "good" or "bad" distract us from being authentically ourselves.

Gilbert did write a follow-up to *Eat, Pray, Love*. "It bombed, and I was fine. Actually, I kind of felt bulletproof, because I knew that I had broken the spell and I had found my way back home to writing for the sheer devotion of it," Gilbert said.[19]

You may view feedback as a lane within which you must perform in order to be accepted. If you receive negative feedback, you may look within and try to figure out what you did wrong. But the true lesson here is that humility takes away the heavy weight of feedback.

While feedback allows you to grow and mature, you can view it more as a data point among a pool of data points. Your choice is what to do with those points.

In Gilbert's case, feedback allows her to refine her craft of writing, but as she eloquently states, "I will always be safe from the random hurricanes of outcome as long as I never forget where I rightfully live."

Use feedback as the contrast to refine your craft, not to define your worth.

---

[19] Jeff Hyman, "Why Humble Leaders Make the Best Leaders," *Forbes*, October 31, 2018, https://www.forbes.com/sites/jeffhyman/2018/10/31/humility/#5bfcc0971c80.

3. Ask for Help

Children are great at asking for help because they know they can't do everything themselves. Sometimes we need to embrace that vulnerability, too. Asking for help requires that we acknowledge we can't do it and are being dependent on someone who can.

You may believe that asking for help is weakness. And, I wouldn't disagree. Reaching out to people in a time of need implies that you can't do it yourself.

In a lot of individualistic cultures, we're taught to hide weaknesses. Especially for young men today, growing up "weak" opens them up to ridicule and isolation. In the professional world, this mindset of "never show weakness" is extremely costly—both in cost efficiency and opportunity costs.

It's time to retrain our brains and become humble leaders. While tempting to do it alone, we can remain confident that asking for help is worthwhile. Everyone has weaknesses—it's what makes us human. We can acknowledge that and not be ashamed to ask for help.

We're born seeking validation from others, and as a result, we too often feel pressured to "put on a show." We're encouraged to weigh our self-worth on what others think of us. And, unfortunately, the pressure to impress and fit in creates toxic work environments and cultures.

Leaders like Jordan Belfort and Regina George might have followers, but it doesn't mean their team dynamics are healthy. In fact, arrogant leadership typically leads to increased levels of judgement, uncertainty, and fear. Worst of all, arrogant leaders create a threatening environment where team members are scared to be themselves.

Your ability to lead via humility creates an atmosphere for creativity and trust, which are benchmarks of productive teams. You now have the strategies to begin growing your humility skill, and it's a choice you can make every day—to be humble or not.

Humility doesn't require that you dismiss all your successes or that you downplay your wins. Instead, it pushes you to love your successes and wins because you want them.

CHAPTER 11
Speaking Doesn't Help You Understand

My teacher used to say, "Silence is golden," and it used to drive me nuts.

Today, I've reversed my judgement. Silence is often an underrated technique that most professionals can use to focus, gain lost momentum, and remain unbiased.

In 2012, Marissa Mayer was named the CEO of Yahoo! After years spent building up Google under the guidance of their leadership team, Mayer felt confident in her ability to turn around the once powerful Yahoo! empire.

Mayer joined Yahoo! with a vision to revamp internal processes and create new revenue opportunities. Days after starting at Yahoo!, Mayer immediately began changing the company. She enforced her new business model while restructuring high-performing teams.

Employees under Mayer provided her with recommendations and strategies to improve the company, but she would not deviate from her plan. Top employees at Yahoo! left in frustration of her leadership style, but this was a price she was willing to pay.

In the midst of the turnaround, Mayer began investing in her personal brand—one of a powerful businesswoman who was innovative and successful. She boasted to popular business publications about the success of her leadership style and the profitability of the company—except, at the time, Mayer wasn't being successful with her Yahoo! turnaround. Instead, it was quite the opposite.

From Mayer's perspective, she needed to be vocal and deliberate. For those working with her, Mayer's authoritarian approach was not effective. Mayer's leadership style was toxic, according to her employees. She didn't listen to feedback. She built walls instead of bridges, and she would spend time bragging about successes that hadn't happened yet.[20]

In 2017, Mayer was removed as CEO of Yahoo! and is a popular case study of what not to do as a leader. Critics to Mayer's approach say that her fatal flaw was talking too much and not listening.

Instead, Mayer needed someone to remind her that silence is golden.

We're stepping into a world that wants us to be vocal. We have more ways than ever before to share our message. In conversations, we're often more focused on what we're going to say next instead of listening to what others have to say.

---

20   Mike Myatt, "Marissa Mayer: A Case Study in Poor Leadership," *Forbes*, November 20, 2015, https://www.forbes.com/sites/mikemyatt/2015/11/20/marissa-mayer-case-study-in-poor-leadership/#6a34723d3b46.

Silence is a tough skill to learn—when to be silent and when to speak up. Marissa Mayer didn't learn that lesson, and it cost her.

The power of silence can benefit you in many ways and allow you to better navigate your work environments and make sustainable impacts.

The four primary uses for silence as a business skill are to:

1. Bring focus back to your task at hand.
2. Better receive feedback from your stakeholders.
3. Allow for more non-biased observation.
4. Gain lost momentum on difficult projects.

1. Returning Focus to Your Current Tasks

We too often have the habit of talking about our successes before we've started them. Consciously or unconsciously, we want to gauge the excitement of those around us in relation to our work. Do my friends think this is cool? Is my grandma going to be proud of me if I work on this? Is what I'm doing any good?

And while this approach is good in the short term, your work shouldn't be created to impress others. It should be done to fulfill you. So, try to not seek validation too early in the process, and just enjoy what you're creating.

By being intentionally silent, you can bring your focus back to your work and allow your task to be the best it can be.

I took this approach while writing this book. With a lot of content being poured into this book, it was very tempting to get my family and friends excited before I was finished. I chose to be intentionally silent about this book to allow me to focus more fully on the end product. Eventually, I will be able to share my accomplishment and be open to their feedback.

If you're doing anything worthwhile, it's more important to invest your full energy in the actual work.

In the case of Mayer, she promoted her accomplishments at Yahoo! before she reached her goals. As a result, every hour she spent talking about her work was an hour taken away from improving the Yahoo! brand.

Eventually, people started to ignore her messaging. She was promoting what she wanted to accomplish; but people want to see results, not what you might do.

The key lesson: Focus on your work and then boast about it once you have something to show.

2. Listening to Feedback

Amid our work process, we should seek feedback from those around us. Sometimes, in our eagerness for feedback, however, we become engaged in a dialogue where we defend our work before anyone has had a chance to critique it. We can try to avoid listening to feedback by searching for an explanation, but that's when we should be silent and absorb—like a sponge.

During a performance review early in my career, my supervisor was giving me feedback on a project that

I had completed. As I sat there, I received positive encouragement about the project, and I was more than happy to sit silently.

Then, when my supervisor began giving me opportunities for the improvement of my performance, I reeled in my head all the of reasons that feedback was wrong.

He also told me I should use more sophisticated budgeting methods. In my head, I was thinking of all the reasons that wasn't possible for this project.

He then advised me to implement more change management frameworks to get the team on my side. I argued that it shouldn't be my job to get other people on board with this clearly necessary project.

In combatting the feedback, I didn't truly learn the necessary lessons.

A couple months later, I made the same mistakes as before. My supervisor once again provided the same feedback.

I sat and listened silently that time, and it was the best feedback I've ever received.

The key lesson: A silent mind can allow more feedback than an active one, and better feedback equals better learning.

3. Allowing for Non-biased Observation

You're expected to take sides on most everything these days. How do you feel about politics? Or religion? Or income inequality? Or climate change?

You're pressured to take sides in business, too. It may manifest as a stereotypical functional tension or as a nuanced internal political struggle. However it appears, silence is a strong solution for remaining nonbiased until you have formed an educated opinion, which is crucial.

As humans, we tend to speak before we think. Then, in an attempt to be right, we back up our opinions with logic that doesn't make sense. Being right, for some people, is more important than being factually correct.

To avoid your fight to be right, be silent and process all the facts before you say a word. Being silent allows you to observe, process, and disseminate data with integrity.

At some point, you will face a situation in which you will be asked to give your opinions or thoughts. For example, you may be in a meeting with a high-level executive who asks you what you think about a new initiative.

Attempting to sound smart, you rattle off some nonsense about how you like the initiative and how it will benefit the company. In reality, you know nothing about the initiative, and you haven't formed an opinion about it.

Instead of seeing your response as wise, the high-level executive dismisses your opinion because he or she can sense your nonsense from a mile away. This scenario happens to professionals all the time, and it hinders your professional growth more than it helps.

From my experience, having an opinion for the sake of

having an opinion is unwise. In situations where you feel pressured to have an opinion, simply say you don't have enough information to decide. It will give you brownie points for not saying the wrong thing, but it also allows you the option to change your mind.

Your approach to silence will need to be intentional.

The key lesson: When in doubt of what you should say, remain silent.

4. Gaining Lost Momentum

You may lose steam on a project over the course of a day or week. It's completely natural.

You exert your energy into your work, and you get the ball rolling. Eventually you run over a small speed bump. And after a couple more speed bumps, you lose your momentum.

Silencing your mind is a great way of regaining your lost momentum.

Strategies like meditation or coffee breaks work well for stopping speed bumps and refocusing your attention. The extra space you create for yourself will allow you to better problem solve and regain your progress.

I recently worked on a project to streamline some company operations. My supervisor tasked me with assessing other departmental processes and aligning my work with theirs to create a streamlined operating model.

At the start, I was scheduling meetings every hour to map our processes. I was meeting with department heads and having great conversations. After a couple days, I had met with everyone and received their input.

As I sat down to map the integrations, I felt extremely disconnected for some reason. I couldn't put the pieces together to create a standard operating procedure, which should've been a simple task. What I realized was that all the meetings I was having wouldn't allow me the time to sit and think about the solutions I wanted to create.

I decided to take a couple minutes and meditate at my desk. It was a simple exercise of silencing my mind and relaxing my thoughts. Once I ended the meditation, I created more space in my brain for conscious thinking to happen.

We need to interact and communicate with our coworkers, but the true value of our thinking comes when we're able to focus completely. And in my case, I was more influenced and distracted by what my coworkers believed I should be doing.

By creating space for myself, I was able to create a solution that benefited everyone—including me.

The key lesson: Silencing your mind is a great strategy for clarifying your perspective and creating more mental space.

As you look at leadership case studies like Marissa Mayer's, you can see that silence, listening, and remaining unbiased are critical skills to succeeding. A strategic use of silence allows you to better lead teams while focusing and receiving feedback.

CHAPTER 12
The Single Secret to Team Success

The most important quality for team success is trust.[21] Whether you're a professional who leads teams or contributes to projects, trust is a critical element of your work. You may think it's a small piece of a larger puzzle, but trust is one of the fundamental building blocks.

Trust is developed between individuals and teams through little acts of kindness and vulnerability over a long period of time. The longer a relationship continues, the more opportunities to build (or erode) trust.

Vulnerability researcher Brené Brown offers a helpful analogy about trust in her book *Daring Greatly* (see also footnote 21). Brown says that each of us has a metaphorical marble jar for each of our relationships. Each time a friend or a teammate acts kindly or contributes to our lives in a positive way, we add a marble to the marble jar. With any act of deceit or duplicity, we take a marble out

---

21 Charles Duhigg, "What Google Learned from Its Quest to Build the Perfect Team," *The New York Times Magazine*, February 25, 2016, https://www.nytimes.com/2016/02/28/magazine/what-google-learned-from-its-quest-to-build-the-perfect-team.html.

of the marble jar.

When you think about those around you, who are your marble jar friends and teammates? Who would you consider part of your support network both at home and at work? Think about how small interactions you share build a stronger bond.

In a professional sense, these acts of trust are simpler than you might think. And, the small investments that you make in your relationships can have major impacts. Over time, these small acts build a stronger bond between team members that allow for more effective performance.

Building Trust

To build a trustworthy reputation, you must be invested in the long term. The healthiest way of developing trust—at work and in life—is to do it exponentially. You start small and work your way up to larger acts over a period of years.

Sometimes you will encounter people who try to build trust at inappropriate rates. Typically, building trust too quickly is a red flag.

A couple years into my career, I reported to a supervisor who built this type of relationship. Having just started working with her, she began to overshare personal information and create a false sense of security. She would often call me on weekends and ask to chat for hours. And, she became very interested in my personal life. I was a little confused as to what she was trying to do. Why was she forcing this trust? As it turned out, she had intended to use me as a pawn in her political game.

The healthiest way to build trust is to do it in small acts. If you're sensing that trust is being forced or built too quickly, there may be ulterior motives.

Think of trust like a seed that you care for. You plant the seed in fresh soil. You feed it and ensure it has proper sunlight. As the plant grows, you water it a little more. Then it starts to take root and you see the first green pop up from the soil.

It wouldn't be appropriate at that point to dump a bucket of water on the plant. You continue watering it lightly until it's able to handle larger amounts of water. You continue to care for the plant moderately, and over the weeks and months and years, it begins to bloom and grow.

Building trust in a relationship is like planting a seed and helping it grow.

When it comes to team dynamics, trust begins with you. If you intend to build trusting relationships, you should not expect others to instigate that trust.

You can begin with small acts of trust, something as simple as doing what you say you're going to do or being honest when a colleague asks for feedback. More examples of acts you can do to build professional trust include the following:

- Set clear expectations

- Communicate early any updates to projects or deadlines
- Keep commitments
- Show up fully present and without distractions
- Stand up for colleagues
- Listen respectfully and without judgement (silence is golden)
- Act with integrity
- Tell the truth
- Own up to your mistakes
- Be inclusive
- Take responsibility for failure
- Avoid gossiping
- Approach team activities with a growth mindset
- Value everyone's opinions equally
- Do what you say
- Say what you mean

This is a short list of how to begin building trust on your team. As you may have noticed, the items on this list require action only on your end. Each of these actions can be done on your own regardless of the circumstances.

As you get into relationships, things become more complex. The items on this list will evolve. It's important to remember that trust, although done in small pieces, is an extremely major foundation of any team. You may not like someone you work with, but it's important to respect and trust them if you plan to be successful.

Rebuilding Trust

You can't be perfect all the time. Sometimes you might slip up and erode trust with coworkers and friends. If you've broken trust with your colleagues or supervisor, it's important to repair that relationship quickly (and genuinely).

Your first step in mending wrongs and rebuilding trust is acknowledging that you've broken that trust. Whether accidently or intentionally, if you've strained a relationship, you'll need to come to terms with that and work to repair it.

The next step after you've identified that you've eroded trust is to apologize. It doesn't matter if you have an excuse or not. What matters is that you're genuinely sorry. This step is hard for us because we're prideful; we hate being wrong.

You may often be tempted to displace the shame or guilt you feel by pawning off the blame onto an external third party. But it's important to own your part.

You'll also need to express interest in continuing the relationship. Depending on how close you are with this individual, you can be up-front with your intention to rebuild trust.

After you've apologized, you can begin rebuilding trust. And, when rebuilding trust, do so with integrity.

Distancing Yourself from Toxic People

In rare cases, you may find toxic or malicious people who take advantage of your trustworthiness in a major way. Sometimes you need to employ a strategy of distancing when working with these people. There are two types of people who may require distancing: cynics and manipulators.

Cynics are easy to spot. Those are the people who outwardly want you to fail. Don't invest time building up trust if that person repeatedly wants you to fail.

Manipulators are trickier. If you're dealing with a manipulator, they will want to create a close bond at first. They find ways of making you feel special, and they build trust at an inappropriate rate. They will then find your passions and weak points. Once they have the information they require, they begin gaslighting and exploiting you in small ways.

My supervisor I mentioned earlier fit into this category. We built trust quickly and our relationship was strong. We both then had moments of breaching trust and rebuilding it. But, after months of this cycle, it occurred to me that she was playing a game. So I had to begin distancing myself from her.

When you begin distancing a relationship, be sure you know what the new relationship should look like. Sometimes your idea of the new relationship is to terminate it all together.

In instances where the relationship needs to continue, you must be more intentional. For example, you may have a coworker or supervisor with whom you need to continue working.

The key to distancing in these relationships is to set distinct and enforceable professional boundaries. Examples of boundaries could include setting working hours and identifying appropriate avenues of communication (i.e., email instead of texting).

Eventually, your boundaries will become the new foundation from which your relationship will grow. At any time, you can reevaluate your boundaries and reset them. Just be sure you have the strength to enforce whatever boundaries you set.

CHAPTER 13
The Lost Art of Conciseness

The average attention span is about eight seconds, so if we want our message to connect, we should get to the point in the clearest way possible without wasting time.

According to Kelton Research's 2018 State of Attention Report, 49 percent of business professionals have said they're more selective about the content they engage with now than they were one year ago.[22] People are getting better at selective listening.

In that same study, Kelton Research discovered that professionals are more distracted than ever before. Ninety-five percent of business professionals said that they multitask during meetings. And, as we continue to fight for attention, the longer we make our communications, the less of our audience we retain in the long run.

The key lesson: Be concise.

---

22 Nadjya Ghausi, "Sorry, Goldfish: People's Attention Spans Aren't Shrinking, They're Evolving," *Entrepreneur*, October 19, 2018, https://www.entrepreneur.com/article/321266.

Principles of Concise Communication

Communicating concisely involves partly science and partly art. You can learn the tricks and tips that help you create professional communications, but truly concise communication comes from ongoing practice.

KNOW YOUR AUDIENCE

In order to be concise, you need to know your audience. Who are you writing or speaking to and what do they care about?

Imagine you're an expert in space aeronautics who has to prepare two presentations—one to the NASA leadership team and one to a sixth-grade science class. Those two audiences care about different things and they each require varying levels of detail and storytelling. Each audience is looking to accomplish a different outcome, and each requires different supporting evidence (photos, stats, etc.) to understand your message.

If you can identify the key priorities that matter to your audience, you'll be able to develop your message accordingly. With the majority of communications you prepare, you'll be able to make inferences about your audience. And, if you don't know, ask.

What are your audience's pain points? What do they care about? What information are they truly looking for? If you know your audience, you'll be able create the one key message you want to communicate.

HAVE ONE KEY MESSAGE

We've all had meetings where we want to squeeze 15 topics into one. If we have the audience, we might as well maximize, so we think. However, we communicate better when we create one key message tailored to our audience.

Using our astronaut example, the sixth-grade class has requested that you come in to share your experience of going into space. Specifically, they're learning about the solar system and planetary orbit.

In this instance, you would not show up to this classroom and talk about orbits, then moon rocks, then Area 51 conspiracy theories. These aren't topics relevant to what they're learning.

The one key message that you create should be relevant to the audience and their needs.

Stay focused.

USE PLAIN LANGUAGE

When we communicate, we assume our audience will understand our point of reference, but they may not. We should always approach communication with plain language, because it's easier to read and understand.

Plain language is a term that refers to basic vocabulary. The more boiled down you can make your message, the easier it is for your audience to digest it. There's not necessarily a list of words that are considered plain language, but always err on the side of basic.

As a caveat, if your target audience requires key vocabulary terms, don't dumb it down. For example, if NASA leadership recognizes the term liquid hydrogen, don't use spaceship juice.

Find familiar words. Be concrete instead of abstract. Use single words instead of circumlocution. Default to short words and sentences.

Plain language also refers to the paragraph and sentence structure you use. Focus on short sentences fewer than 20 words. Any sentences longer than 20 words and you'll lose people.

STRUCTURE YOUR COMMUNICATION

You know your audience, and you know your key message. Now you need to structure the communication.

In what format is your communication—written, oral, or video? Once you know the format, you can plan your structure a little more effectively.

You will want to state your message clearly—don't bury the lede. What makes your story newsworthy to your audience?

Next, you'll want to back up your message with supporting information. This could be data, details, or stories. Your supporting information should always be relevant to your audience.

Presenting to executives? They probably don't care about every detail. Emailing your supervisor? They probably don't need full anecdotes.

In most communications, you can start with this basic structure:

1. Summarize what you're going to tell them.
2. Tell them.
3. Restate what you've told them.

No matter the format, your structure should be easily understood and relevant to your audience.

BE CRITICAL OF CONTENT

As you begin drafting your communication, be critical. The content you produce is important, but not all your content is important to everyone.

Once you've developed your communication, spend time editing it. You should aim to keep your sentences short and your message clear. Ask yourself a series of questions to help you tighten your communication.

Is this sentence/paragraph necessary to the understanding of the document? Can I say this in a shorter/clearer way? Are these sentences/paragraphs too long? Does this sentence/picture support the message or detract from it? Is any of this information naturally implied?

Take a red pen to your work. Your audience will thank you.

The Art of Conciseness

I could drag this chapter out further, but that would contradict my point.

We're all strapped for time, and in professional settings, conciseness may be the difference between your ideas getting implemented or scrapped.

Improving your communication must be a focused effort. To make the impact you want on your audience, be clear and be concise. Be intentional in your communication and improve where you can. By knowing your audience and using plain language, you can better convey your message.

The key lesson: Communicate concisely, because eight seconds goes by quickly.

CHAPTER 14
The Cowardly Lion

The Wizard of Oz, the 1939 movie adapted from L. Frank Baum's children's book, is one of the most memorable films ever created.

It tells the story of Dorothy, a Kansas girl who befriends the Scarecrow, the Tin Man, and the Cowardly Lion as she attempts to get home.

The character of the Cowardly Lion has always fascinated me. He's got sharp teeth, a massive roar, and a large mane. But the giant lion is scared of his own shadow.

On a mission to end his cowardice, the lion seeks out the Medal of Courage, which can be bestowed only by the Wizard of Oz. Once acquired, this medal would allow the lion to do anything with outstanding bravery. The Wizard gives the lion the medal, and he miraculously becomes courageous. But to no one's surprise, we see that the lion's courage wasn't in the medal. His courage was inside of him the whole time.

We carry our courage, too.

We're all professional creators—whether it's art, music, or spreadsheets. We create something new every day. When we create, we open ourselves up to criticism, feedback, and praise. And unfortunately, sometimes that fear of criticism or judgement keeps us in cowardice.

I encountered a major "Cowardly Lion" moment early on in my career. I had a great team and a high-profile position at a global company. I had been at the company for three years, and I was itching for a promotion.

After weeks of positive self-talk, I scheduled a meeting with my supervisor. He had always been supportive and encouraging of my growth, yet I still felt extremely nervous. I walked into the room with clammy hands and weak shaky legs.

"What's up?" my supervisor asked.

"I just... uh... wanted to chat," I said.

The meeting went on. When it came time for me to make the pitch, I shied away. I asked for a compensation raise, but I didn't have the guts to fight for the promotion. Feeling like I had failed, I replayed the conversation repeatedly trying to find where I went wrong.

At any defining moment, we're faced with two choices—cowardice or courage. And far too often, we unconsciously choose cowardice.

In my case, my cowardice was the result of a fear of rejection. We face moments like this every day—not all of them as major. But we put ourselves on the line, and we face the decision of either cowardice or courage.

The big question is: How can we more *intentionally* choose courage in difficult situations?

Our ability to choose courage over cowardice is directly related to how comfortable we are with embracing vulnerability. As Dr. Brené Brown says in her book *Daring Greatly,* vulnerability is "uncertainty, risk, and emotional exposure" in any situation.[23]

"Our inability to lean into the discomfort of vulnerability limits the fullness of those important experiences that are wrought with uncertainty: Love, belonging, trust, joy, and creativity to name a few," Brown says.

While vulnerability makes us uneasy, it's also a requirement if we ever hope to accomplish anything worthwhile. When we lean into vulnerability, that's courage.

Every defining courageous decision in business was made by *vulnerable* leaders:

Tim Cook taking over Apple after Steve Job's death

Oprah Winfrey walking away from a successful TV show to launch her network

Bob Iger's decision to buy Marvel, Pixar, and Lucasfilm

Not one of these people was able to have courage without embracing vulnerability. This is a small list of the leaders who have shown extreme acts of vulnerability and courage.

---

23 Brené Brown, Ph.D., L.M.S.W., "Myth: 'Vulnerability Is a Weakness,'" *Oprah*, March 14, 2013, http://www.oprah.com/own-super-soul-sunday/excerpt-daring-greatly-by-dr-brene-brown.

Our willingness to show up fully in our work is a choice. We're always wearing our own Medal of Courage, and that courage can lead to a more fulfilling life—if we let it.

To help you more consciously show up in your work, you can use these four strategies.

1. Hold Yourself Accountable

One of the most daunting vulnerability exercises is taking accountability for your actions.

You may have been in a situation where *someone* does something wrong on a project. And instead of owning up that the *someone* was you, you play dumb. While there may be no visible harm in playing dumb, the courageous response would be to own up.

As you get into the habit of owning your part, you will stop blaming others (which is the real goal here). Instead of spending a lot of time pointing fingers and demanding that others perform differently, you need to take accountability for your own role. It's a vulnerable place to be, but owning your part gives you the control to change the outcome.

2. Create a Support Network

Being vulnerable means that sometimes you won't get the outcome you want. And that's okay.

When you start living more courageously, make sure you have a strong support network to catch you if you fall. Your support network should include five or six people you trust most—they could be your supervisors, family members, friends, partners, and mentors.

Your support network is there to cheer you on when you're winning, and dust you off when you fall.

3. Know You're in the Arena

It is not the critic who counts; not the man who points out how the strong man stumbles, or where the doer of deeds could have done them better. The credit belongs to the man who is actually in the arena, whose face is marred by dust and sweat and blood; who strives valiantly; who errs, who comes short again and again, because there is no effort without error and shortcoming; but who does actually strive to do the deeds; who knows great enthusiasms, the great devotions; who spends himself in a worthy cause; who at the best knows in the end the triumph of high achievement, and who at the worst, if he fails, at least fails while daring greatly, so that his place shall never be with those cold and timid souls who neither know victory nor defeat.

—Theodore Roosevelt, April 1910, "Citizenship in a Republic" Speech

When you take on any uncertain endeavor, you enter the arena, where you can expect to be kicked and beat down. You also expect those sitting in the cheap seats to tell you how you could do better. To those critics, I turn to Brené Brown.

A lot of cheap seats in the arena are filled with people who never venture onto the floor. They just hurl mean-spirited criticisms and put-downs from a safe distance.... But when we're defined by what people think, we lose

the courage to be vulnerable. Therefore, we need to be selective about the feedback we let into our lives. ***For me, if you're not in the arena also getting your ass kicked, I'm not interested in your feedback.***

—Brené Brown, *Rising Strong: The Reckoning. The Rumble. The Revolution*

When you choose to be courageous, you're in a select pool of gladiators. You should be interested in the feedback of those who are also getting their asses kicked because that feedback has more merit and validity.

Ignore the haters.

4. Focus on the Butterflies

We pursue vulnerable situations to find joy and happiness. That excitement feels like butterflies. Then, when vulnerability sets in, those butterflies can turn into rocks.

Let the joy and excitement carry you. Your vulnerability will stick with you until you reach success. In the meantime, find that excitement and use it like jet fuel. It's easier said than done, but it's doable if you're intentional about your focus.

As you begin building your amazing career, you'll run into defining moments where you can either choose courage or cowardice. If you're destined to live your best life, you need to have the courage to show up and make it happen, and to wear that medal proudly.

CHAPTER 15
The More Lives You Live, The More Empathy You Gain

Empathy is like a muscle, and it needs to be exercised regularly for your team to reach its peak success. You strengthen your empathy—the ability to put yourself in someone else's shoes—as a natural consequence of living. The more you're exposed to life, the more consciously aware you are of others' experiences. And with those experiences, you tone and shape your empathy.

Empathizing isn't about judging people's goodness; it's about accepting what makes them human. Connecting with humanity forces you to put down your walls and see others' experiences with understanding eyes. You have the opportunity every day to display understanding instead of judgement. Each experience you live widens your definition of humanity.

Empathy allows you to better lead your teams, and research also shows that leaders who manage empathetically can increase overall team loyalty and employee satisfaction. The Center for Creative Leadership, a leadership education provider, says that empathetic leaders improve their team's overall performance more than apathetic leaders.[24]

As the research shows, empathy improves performance across the world, regardless of culture, but contingent mostly on power distance. High power distance cultures value a formal hierarchy and respect strong reporting structures. Low power distance cultures are more informal and are typically structured more democratically.

For high power distance cultures like those in Asian countries, empathically led teams will outperform competitors significantly. In countries with low power distance like the United States, the difference in performance will be less than with high power distance cultures, but still significant.

Where Does Empathy Come From?

Scientifically speaking, empathy comes from our brains, specifically from the *right supramarginal gyrus,* which is part of the cerebral cortex.[25]

By default, our brains are hardwired to project our emotional state onto others. But the right supramarginal gyrus allows us to diverge from that hardwiring and assess another's emotional state without projecting our own baggage.

---

[24] William A. Gentry, Todd J. Weber, and Golnaz Sadri, "Empathy in the Workplace, A Tool for Effective Leadership," *Center for Creative Leadership White Paper,* 2016, http://www.ccl.org/wp-content/uploads/2015/04/EmpathyInTheWorkplace.pdf.

[25] Christopher Bergland, "The Neuroscience of Empathy," *Psychology Today,* October 10, 2013, https://www.psychologytoday.com/us/blog/the-athletes-way/201310/the-neuroscience-empathy.

If given time to process, we can control our emotional projections in a lot of situations. But most situations don't have processing time. So for rapid-fire thinking, we pull on previously established *neural networks*.

Those neural networks are established by our previous life experiences, and they create shortcut responses that help us process the world faster. It's sort of like our brain's speed-dial response (for those of you who know what speed dial is).

Our brains are inherently lazy. Although we have the ability to assess another's emotional state objectively, our brains would much rather use neural networks. As a result, most of our emotional responses are preprogramed.

For example, if I were to show you a video of someone slamming their finger in a car door, your brain could do two things.

The first option: It could objectively look at the situation and assess all contributing factors to determine that slamming a finger in a door hurts a lot.

The second option: Your brain will think back to the time you slammed your finger in something, and it would activate your preestablished neural networks. You watch the incident happen to someone else, and you might even feel your finger hurt slightly. That's your previous neural networks at work. It's faster and takes less energy.

Our brains are trained to react emotionally based on our previous experiences. The more experiences we have, the more data our brains rely on to understand others.

The better we can understand others, the more empathy we can feel. And, because our brains' neural networks are constantly changing, our ability to empathize can get stronger through mindful focus. We can intentionally rewire our brains to be more empathic.

How Can You Strengthen Your Empathy Muscle?

If you're looking for conscious growth, you can try the following strategies.

1. Seek New Experiences

You likely create *content bubbles*, or *spheres of influence*, in your life that keep you in your comfort zone. You read the news you like, follow the social media accounts that match your personality, and watch the shows that reflect your beliefs.

If you're looking to increase your empathy, add diversity into your content bubbles. It will give you more insight into other stories and experiences that you wouldn't have experienced otherwise.

For example, I am a 6'4" single white male. I read a working mothers blog for a couple of months as part of this strategy. Was it at all relevant to my day-to-day experience? Not really, but I learned so much about what matters to working mothers—such as how stressful it is to find a daycare center that is reliable, cost-effective, and open until 6 p.m., or how to manage a full schedule with a sick child.

While I myself don't need to find a daycare, it shifted my perspective. I no longer get annoyed when a coworker needs to cancel a meeting last minute to go pick up a sick child from school.

By diversifying your content bubble, you begin to experience more empathy for that diverse group.

You can easily find content outside your content bubbles. All you have to do is search. The following table shows examples of new content bubbles you could jump into.

Content Bubble	Example of Application
Functional Bubble	I'm a marketing professional, but I'll read blogs about human resources.
Experience Bubble	I'm a junior employee, but I'll read CEO news and reports.
Geography Bubble	I live in the United States, but I'll watch news from the United Kingdom.
Gender Bubble	I identify as male, but I can read more about non-binary issues.
Sexual Orientation Bubble	I'm straight, but I'll consume more about LGBTQ and business.

The key is to know how you identify and find resources that are outside of that scope. You don't necessarily have to agree with every piece of content, but you should approach it nonjudgmentally.

2. Be Aware of Your Responses

Empathy is about putting yourself in someone else's shoes, but in order to do that, you need to be self-aware of your own emotions first.

If you're approached with a problem, you may be tempted to take on that problem's negative energy as your own. Be aware of which emotions belong to you and which do not.

Being empathetic doesn't mean you need to be consumed by others' emotions. It means that you should be able to acknowledge them and navigate them without judgement.

For example, if I slam my finger in a door, you shouldn't be screaming in pain with me. Instead, you should recognize the pain and find me an ice pack ASAP.

Your response to a situation is an important indicator to others of your emotional intelligence and empathy. In most professional situations, the most empathetic response you can have is to listen silently. Don't underestimate the power of just being present with no other action required.

3. Know Your Unconscious Biases

Knowing your biases might be one of the toughest strategies to use, but circumventing unconscious biases will allow you to be more present in a situation so that you can navigate more clearly. Once you become aware of your biases, you will be able to navigate around them.

One type of bias that some people have is a *hiring bias*. We typically like to hire people who are like us. For example, I'm an extrovert, so I tend to get along best with other extroverts. If I'm aware of this bias, I will be able to go into interviews without judging through that lens. That is to say that if I'm interviewing someone who isn't an extrovert, I shouldn't be judgmental of his or her introverted personality traits.

You can find biases a couple different ways. You can research common biases or ask for feedback from your colleagues.

4. Challenge Your Assumptions

Lastly, challenge your assumptions. You build neural networks to help yourself think more quickly, but sometimes those neural networks run in the background and you may not even notice. If you have strong beliefs, be willing to challenge them. You don't have to *change* them, but you should be comfortable exploring them.

For example, right after college, I moved to New York City. I had tons of assumptions about what NYC was (and wasn't). I had thoughts such as "people are rude" or "it's so expensive."

Once I began experiencing the city, I noticed that not everyone is rude and not everything is expensive. After challenging my assumptions, I was able to create new beliefs that allowed me to view the city with optimistic whimsy instead of guarded curiosity.

In a more professional setting, we make assumptions about all kinds of things. We have beliefs about companies, industries, and functions. For a long time, I had major assumptions about how disorganized all startups were. Then, after mingling with entrepreneurs and working with startups, I learned to appreciate the organized chaos. I can now empathize with that world.

Our ability to empathize with team members gives us the ability to lead our team effectively in any context. We can choose to embrace our experiences and become more emotionally aware, thus making our teams and ourselves stronger and more connected.

CHAPTER 16
The Real "You"

"Just be yourself."

When anyone gives us that advice, it implies authenticity and it assumes self-comfortableness. Honestly, when people tell me to just be myself, I have no idea what being myself looks like.

A Japanese proverb states that we all have three masks. The first mask we show to the world, the second we show to our families, and the last we never show to anyone. The third mask is said to be our most authentic self.

Which mask should I wear if I'm being myself?

There's some debate about how to interpret the proverb. Some say we betray ourselves if we're anything but authentic. Others say each mask represents a unique piece of us, and we share those pieces with the world when appropriate.

I think the interpretation lies somewhere in between. I believe we define who we are in every moment by how we act, what we believe, and who we aspire to be. The masks we show the world are truly who we are, but those masks are ever-changing.

Authenticity is the culmination of our beliefs, values, past experiences, and aspirations. And we all wish to be authentic. But our authenticity is constantly being challenged, tested, and changed.

Typically, we measure our level of authenticity based on how comfortable we are in any situation. The less comfortable we feel, the less authentic we believe ourselves to be.

For example, let's say you're laid-back, and you love casual work environments. You prefer jeans and sneakers all day every day. Now you have a big job interview coming up. For that interview, you've decided to wear a nice suit and tie or a nice skirt and blouse—standard interview attire.

As you get ready for your interview, you say things like, "Ugh, I hate ties because they're too tight" or "I never wear heels. This feels so wrong." In this moment, you may think formal business attire is not authentically you because it's uncomfortable.

In another example, you're an introverted data analyst. You get a promotion to a new role that requires you to manage people. You prefer to communicate using data and technical information to ensure no miscommunications, and you prefer to communicate via email.

The direct reports on your team don't have the same

technical background as you and ask you to change your communication style to help them understand better. They want less email and more dialogue. Changing your communication style is necessary for your team, but it feels uncomfortable to you. In this example, you'd most likely think that less data and fewer emails is inauthentic to who you are.

In situations that test your authenticity, you judge your "self-ness" on your previous experiences and comfort level, i.e., you've always wore jeans and that's part of your identity. Wearing formal attire therefore feels inauthentic.

Take the pressure off yourself. What typically holds us back is our **limiting beliefs**, or expectations of who we *should* be. We create narratives about ourselves as we learn and grow, and sometimes, we experience stark contrast to that narrative (jeans vs. suit) that challenges our existing one.

So, what does this mean for you as a professional? You will encounter moments in your professional life that make you question your authenticity. *Am I being true to myself?*

The short answer is that you will always be true to yourself—no matter what you do. To intentionally uncover the most authentic response for your situation, you will need find your limiting beliefs.

You likely carry self-limiting identities that prevent you from creating your butterfly-filled career. Your ability to own your authenticity is dependent first on your willingness to change your narrative.

If you're currently experiencing an authenticity crisis, here are some steps to help you create the right response that's authentically you. I call this the Redefining Authenticity Process.

1. Identify Your Narrative.
2. Uncover Your Limiting Beliefs.
3. Own Your Story.

Step One: Identify Your Narrative

Your narrative comes from your beliefs, past experiences, and ambitions. In defining your narrative, you're constantly defining your identity and shifting your comfort zone to match what you believe to be true about yourself.

Take a few minutes to think through your narrative. How would you describe yourself? What events have shaped you as a professional? Do you like your career? Why or why not? Where do you see yourself in five years?

Part of identifying your narrative is discovering the sources for your identity. Some come from your experiences, ambitions, and the strengths inventories that you did in chapter 5. Other parts of your identity come from mirroring—how others reflect your identity back to you.

Social media is one tool we use to mirror. We use platforms like Instagram, Facebook, and LinkedIn to crowdsource our identities. We engage and interact with whatever makes us comfortable, and that helps our perspective. With that cycle of trial and error, we offer prototypes of our personalities to see how they're received.

To show you how this Redefining Authenticity exercise works, I'm going to use myself as an example. In this example, I've created a short professional narrative about myself.

> My name is Ben Preston. I'm a laid-back, young marketing professional who loves traveling and writing. I'm talented at client engagement, process improvement, and strategy development. I'm not passionate about finance or IT, but I enjoy the data analysis that overlaps those two functions.

As I grow professionally, elements of my narrative will be reinforced or dismantled, and that's how I will articulate my authenticity. If you notice, there's items in my narrative that will limit me as I grow, and that's okay for now. I'll talk more about navigating that later.

Step Two: Uncover Your Limiting Beliefs

The next step in redefining your authenticity is understanding what limiting beliefs might keep you from succeeding. In everyday life, you may not need to change your limiting beliefs. Typically, you'll need to tackle your limiting beliefs if you're experiencing change or you're hitting a ceiling.

Before we get into the example, you should understand what limiting beliefs are and how they might affect your career. In a broad sense, limiting beliefs are thoughts or values you hold that prevent you from succeeding at your goals or ambitions.

Generally, most of your beliefs will not limit you. For example, if you believe that marketing and sales should work together, that belief will rarely limit your ability to succeed. As you start to grow professionally, however, you will run up against some dusty beliefs you're going to have to change.

Once you've identified your limiting beliefs, you'll be able to intentionally change them to create a more seamless success path. Another way to say this would be, "Get rid of beliefs that no longer *serve* you." You'll continue being authentically you, but you'll be less resistant about it.

Going back to my example from earlier, let's say that I'm getting a promotion from individual contributor to manager of a team. I'll underline any limiting beliefs I might have in my example that would prevent me from being authentic in my management.

After rereading my narrative:

> My name is Ben Preston. I'm a laid-back, **young** marketing professional who loves traveling and writing. **I'm talented at client engagement, process improvement, and strategy development. I'm not passionate about Finance or IT,** but I enjoy the data analysis that overlaps those two functions.

You may have caught more than what I've underlined here, but I want to focus on three common limiting beliefs that we run into: classification, projection, and distancing.

The first common limiting belief is self-classification. In this example, I have classified myself as young. "Young" implies that I'm inexperienced or that age has a weighing factor on my work. We can classify ourselves in multiple ways—age, industry, function, etc. While classifications have a place, the stereotypes associated with them often hold us back if we believe them too strongly. In my example, I can be young and successful, but I should be cautious not to let my classification define what I'm capable of achieving.

The second common limiting belief is projection. We talked about projecting in chapter 15, and this is a similar concept. Projection is when we assume others have similar beliefs or the same interests as we do. In my example, I say I'm great at client engagement, process improvement, and strategy development. My excitement in these areas isn't limiting at all. However, as I grow, I should be aware that my bias is strategy development, but my team might not be good at strategy development. I can't project my experience onto my team.

The third common limiting belief is distancing. Distancing is common when we're unfamiliar with or lack empathy for a group of people. The belief that a group is "bad" will cloud our judgement and cause us to treat the people in that group differently. In my case, I've distanced myself from finance and IT. If left unchanged, my belief will create inherently negative interactions.

Taking all that feedback into consideration, I need to change some limiting beliefs before I begin leading a team. Here's my revised statement:

> My name is Ben Preston. I'm a laid-back marketing professional who loves traveling and writing.

> I get excited about client engagement, process improvement, and strategy development. I look forward to managing a diverse team with unique strengths. I also enjoy data analysis and how we can better use it to improve our functions across the company.

Now, I've shifted my limiting beliefs to something more positive while remaining authentic to who I am. While both statements are authentic to me, the second one allows me to succeed more fully without running into a ceiling.

Step Three: Own Your Story

The last step to redefining your authenticity is to own your narrative through action. You can spend time rewriting your authenticity narrative, but if you don't act, it doesn't really matter. Your identity is no longer limited by your previous story, so celebrate your growth-oriented self.

In my case, I can continue to be excited by my strengths, and I can continue exploring my preferred methods of management. For example, I might begin collaborating with finance and IT. While I'm not strong in either of those functions, I can empathize with their work and tie in their strengths to my team. Also, my acknowledgement of a diverse team means I can now authentically test new communication styles and management techniques.

The process of owning your new narrative takes time. It's not as simple as flipping a light switch. You may slip into your old beliefs, but the goal is to embrace your new frame of mind.

THE REAL "YOU"

The business world is constantly changing, and in order to succeed, you'll need to adapt, too. Your authenticity is defined by you, and you're able to change it whenever you want to adapt your situation.

CHAPTER 17
Quarter-Life Crisis

We put a lot of pressure on our careers. We need them to provide income, stability, and fulfillment. So, when we get the right job that meets our criteria, we feel amazing! We feel like we're in perfect alignment with who we're *supposed* to be. Our futures are limitless, we think.

Although on the outside we've reached our superficial success, on the inside we may still feel a layer of discontentment.

In June 2015, I had just celebrated my 23rd birthday. Another year older, another year wiser. My life was how I'd dreamed it to be. I had the perfect job. I lived in New York City. I got to travel the world. My friends were fantastic. And I was playing basketball at least three times a week.

Everything was *perfect*.

Yet, as I looked around, I felt disconnected and depressed. While my life was textbook perfect, I couldn't shake this feeling of dissatisfaction.

A couple weeks passed, and I was still in a slump. I consulted friends and coworkers trying to get to the root of my discontent.

Then it hit me like a punch to my gut. I couldn't breathe. I curled into a fetal position trying to hold back tears. The plain white walls of my tiny apartment started closing in. I was experiencing a paralyzing panic attack.

After what felt like hours, I started breathing normally again. I sat up and slowly regained control. *What the f*ck was that?* I remember thinking.

Only after months of self-reflection did I understand what this anxiety attack was. I had had a full-on quarter-life crisis.

The Purpose of Anxiety

We're blessed with emotions that act as indicator gauges, just as a car has status lights to give us insight as to what's happening under the hood.

Anxiety is like our bodies' Check Engine light. We create an idealized version of what our career should look like, and we feel superficially happy. Then, we get a Check Engine warning in the form of dissatisfaction or discontent.

Like most drivers, we ignore the Check Engine light because we think it's probably nothing. We keep driving our careers and distract ourselves from the blinking light. "It'll work itself out," we reassure ourselves. We put another 10,000 miles on our careers until one day the engine explodes. And we find ourselves curled up in a fetal position on our cheap Ikea mattress.

Anxiety suggests that we need to check under the hood before we keep driving. Specifically, it's an indicator light that we're not aligned with our inner purpose. Our logic says we're fine, but our anxiety says the opposite.

So, the next logical question is, "What do I do about it?"

Regain Your Footing

When faced with adversity, we all have unique ways of coping. The very first thing you should do when your engine explodes is to get grounded.

A common and effective grounding exercise is the **5-4-3-2-1 Method:**

5: Acknowledge **five** things you see around you.
4: Acknowledge **four** things you can touch around you.
3: Acknowledge **three** things you hear.
2: Acknowledge **two** things you can smell.
1. Acknowledge **one** thing you can taste.

This exercise is intended to bring you into the present. Anxiety often happens when you're too worried about the future, so focusing your attention on the present levels your emotional state.

Ideally, your next step would be to begin building your new future. But, in my experience, you can rarely go from a "super negative" place to a "super positive" place with the snap of your fingers. So, take the time to get yourself into a positive space before you start planning.

One method that gets me into a happier, positive place is applying gratitude and appreciation. Usually, we're grateful when life is good. When everything is going our way, we're thankful for all the gifts and opportunities we've been presented.

Applying gratitude is one of the most effective methods of getting you from crappy to happy relatively quickly. Find things in your life to be grateful for. They don't even have to be major. They can be whatever makes you feel better about where you are at this moment.

"I'm grateful to have a supportive family. I'm glad I'm financially stable. I'm happy I'm healthy and breathing. I'm grateful that my emotions are working properly. I appreciate the opportunity to create a more fulfilling life for myself."

Just keep finding the things that you appreciate, and after a couple minutes, you'll be in a much better headspace to begin planning your future.

Create a New Timeline

After you've cleared your head, you can begin planning the roadmap back to an exciting career—one that gives you butterflies.

I call this process starting a new timeline. At any point

in your life, you have the ability to start over, to create a new timeline.

The process for this can be as simple or as complicated as you want to make it. Identify what fueled your anxiety. What's your Check Engine light asking you to evaluate? If you're not sure what caused it, that's okay. Sometimes anxiety is caused by things outside the workplace, so evaluate that as well.

Your anxiety is personal to you, but some possible causes are:

- Dissatisfaction with your current job
- Feeling that your career won't take you where you want to go (a.k.a. feeling trapped)
- Being inadequate in comparison to those around you
- Lack of community or social impact in your role

This list includes some common work-related reasons. Once you've identified yours, start thinking how you want to approach creating a new timeline.

If you are risk-averse, you might want to change one small thing at a time. If you're not risk-averse, like me, you might want to go all-in to change, and that's okay, too.

Start by answering the following questions:

- Who do I want to be a year from now?
- What makes me excited to go to work?
- With all the opportunities to learn, what skills will help me in my desired career?

- If I don't know my career path yet, what are one or two things I can do to clarify that?

Once you start answering those basic questions, you'll gain some momentum and have some ideas for your new timeline.

In my case, I realized that I didn't want to be in communications anymore, and I wanted a function that was more ROI oriented. I also discovered that I get excited by opportunities that challenge my strategic problem-solving skills. Lastly, I realized that I didn't like New York City as much as I had thought.

My self-discovery, while it may seem small, gave me some much-needed clarity on my career path:

1. I needed to research new functions outside of communications.
2. I needed to find jobs that had more strategic-thinking opportunities.
3. I needed to take an inventory of what I wanted in a city.

I also had actionable steps I could take to improve my situation. And while my situation didn't transform overnight, I was able to work toward a future that made me excited again.

Looking back at my quarter-life crisis, I'm happy I had that transformative experience. In the moment, it sucked, but I think we all need to experience those anxiety attacks sometimes to wake us from complacency.

I believe we're all destined to do great things in the

world, and without internal nudges, we wouldn't be motivated to change. We need to make sure we pay attention if our Check Engine light comes on.

CHAPTER 18
Impact Starts with You

As professionals we look at the world and see opportunities to make it better—for everyone. But how can we influence change in our organizations that will activate our businesses to do good? We don't have to be a CEO to make a difference; we just have to be creative. We're surrounded by opportunities to make an impact within our current roles.

My good friend Alicia Case leads a Business Resource Group (BRG)—known as Égalité—in her organization for LGBTQ+ employees and their allies. The group focuses on LGBTQ+ employees, advocating for internal company policy changes that benefit LGBTQ+ employees, educating the organization on LGBTQ+ issues and topics, and making a more equitable workplace for LGBTQ+ employees and all marginalized groups.

The BRG started out as a networking group to gather LGBTQ+ employees around a common cause, and quickly took its energy toward favorable LGBTQ+ internal policies, and fundraising for nonprofits benefiting the LGBTQ+ community. Then, the group harnessed the power of its members for even greater good. The Chicago Chapter of the BRG rallied its members together to create a pro bono awareness campaign—known as PrEP4Love—to shine a light on the use of PrEP—a medication used to stop the transmission and spread of HIV during sex. This was a fantastic example of how a group of purposed-driven employees could have an even greater impact outside of the walls of their offices and support the local Chicago LGBTQ+ community.

The group's work has made a huge and lasting impact. As a result, Égalité created a more equitable, diverse, and inclusive workforce; donated more than $650,000 to charity; and launched an awareness campaign to prevent the transmission and spread of HIV. The BRG made an impact in my friend's community and business, and she created career fulfillment for herself.

Another good friend of mine, Lori DePace, aimed to make an impact using the program she oversees. DePace started at her company supporting the talent acquisition team as a coordinator.

Wanting to create social impact for the interns and herself, DePace expanded her role from general TA support to supporting the internship program. She felt that she could use her skills to help young professionals find their passions, and she could aid them in reaching their goals.

As DePace began working on the intern program, she saw it as a bigger opportunity than just placing interns into a position. DePace and her team supported interns throughout the duration of their internship through programming. This programming allowed interns to network with high-level executives, uncover their strengths, and find more purposeful work.

After years of refining the intern program, DePace and her team have transformed a simple summer internship program into an opportunity for young professionals to expand their technical skillsets and discover their purpose at the same time.

Her work continues to provide social impact to this day. Her program was recognized as one of the Top 100 Internship Programs in the U.S. by WayUp (two years in a row). DePace and her team maintain a strong conversion rate of intern to full-time hire, which at the time of writing this book is above 50 percent.

DePace and Case aren't CEOs, but they both made major impacts that elevated their companies and served a social good.

But how do you do it? How do you take a for-profit company's resources and apply them toward a social cause while still meeting your goals? How can you, too, have a win for you and a win for your company?

Four Levels of Advocacy

I've broken down corporate advocacy into four parts. You can think of these as participation levels. As you move up the advocacy ladder, you'll need to develop more creative solutions than in the early levels.

1. OBSERVER

The necessary stage for all movers and shakers is observing. What is the problem? How do you feel about it? What's being done outside and inside your company to improve that issue?

For the sake of this process, let's use environmental sustainability as the problem you're observing. You might see which recycling and paperless initiatives are currently implemented. You might notice the key drivers of the programs and unique challenges those individuals face.

You may also consider how your company culture does when presented with social change initiatives. How do your colleagues and leadership team respond to change?

For DePace and Case, their organizations supported social initiatives and encouraged grassroots activism.

2. PASSIVE SUPPORTER

After you've scoped the playing field, you may decide to be a passive supporter. You can't lead every cause, but you can support them. Passive supporters might make up 85 percent of participants for social causes.

In the case of environmental sustainability, passive supporters would be the people you encourage to recycle or use less paper. Depending on what you're asking of them, they might donate during fundraising events or pledge in the case of a petition.

For Case, passive supporters donated to her fundraisers. For DePace, passive supporters were the managers and team members of the interns. Neither Case nor DePace asked their supporters to go above and beyond, but they did ask for their support.

The bulk of passive supporters will support your cause without hesitation if you're not asking them to do too much.

3. ACTIVE SUPPORTER

Active supporters are the people who support your vision and want to take a direct role in making a difference. Think of active supporters as the key influencers and team members you need to rely on to make your social cause a success.

This group may be different for every cause, so you'll have to be creative. In DePace's initiative, her active supporters were her manager and the executive team. For Case, it was her BRG team and the client they were working for.

Most organizations won't readily allow teams or committees to form around a social cause unless there is a business case to do so. At this point, start thinking about how your business case can benefit the company.

In our example of environmental sustainability, laying out the company benefits can be tricky. Perhaps the paperless initiative will result in lower overhead costs. If you run fundraising events, you can position them as employee engagement opportunities. Or, if you want to start something big like a BRG, you can work with the marketing/PR team to publicize the initiative since corporate sustainability is a big talking point these days.

You'll have to get creative with your pitch to your executives. Once you get the right angle, the benefits can be huge.

4. LEADER

Once you've got the ball rolling, you're a leader of a movement. This is when the fun happens. You've got the company on your side and employee support. Now, you can assess where the future of the cause is moving and shape it.

DePace uses her impact to recruit new purpose-driven interns to the company, and it's a huge selling point which leads to better retention. Case leads Egalité to lead pro bono campaigns, donate more than $650,000 to LGBTQ+ charities, and create a more inclusive workplace.

To be a leader, you need to have a vision. How can you mobilize your initiative to bring more revenue into the company, lead the industry, or make your organization more marketable?

Companies like LEGO or Walmart would be good role models to show how big environmental sustainability can be within organizations. LEGO is running completely renewable and is now researching new materials for making LEGOs (like bamboo plastic) that would save the company money. Walmart challenged its vendors to grow more organic food options for customers, and the company now markets those products at low prices.

The sky is the limit for what impact you can make. To be successful, you'll want to grow organically. Don't try and take it from zero to 60 too quickly.

Finding Your Voice

Every level of advocacy is equally respectable. I used to think that I needed to be passionate about every cause all the time. The truth is, being an advocate for everything is exhausting, and you rarely can give your all. If you're looking to be an active supporter or leader of a cause in your workplace, focus on one or two. Your full attention has much more impact if you're focused. Spreading yourself too thin won't make a dent anywhere.

If you're itching to make an impact in your organization, be sure to research your opportunities. You might have an idea already of what you want to do, and that's great! If you have no idea, that's okay, too. Feel out what you're passionate about and bring that to the office.

For example, I have a strong interest in indoor plants, and I wanted to make our office more plant friendly. I got a stipend from our executive team to order office plants, and I take care of them. Our team's mental health has improved, and the air is less toxic.

Or, if you're a huge animal lover, perhaps you can bring in animals from a local shelter once a month for an adoption event. Your coworkers could play with puppies and kittens, and some of them might even adopt an animal.

Whatever your cause is, you don't have to go outside work to support it. Make your business more socially minded. It will make you more engaged at work, and your coworkers will be excited at the opportunity to make a difference.

If you do start a social movement at your office, I'd love to hear about it! Send me an email or LinkedIn message with what you did and how successful it was.

Epilogue

You've arrived at the end of the book. When you started this journey, you were looking for the confidence and strength to build an exciting career. Now, I hope you feel ready to take on the world.

We all want a career that lights us up inside—that gives us butterflies. I believe we're all meant to have fulfilling careers and do what we love. Finding your perfect job isn't impossible; it just requires that you follow your butterflies.

Going back to the analogy in chapter 1, having an exciting career is like playing a game of darts. Many of us aim for a 15-point career when we deserve a perfect bullseye. Now you have the confidence to make it happen.

Along the journey, you've learned how to hack your motivation and find your strengths. You understand the value of your attention and how to remain resilient through adversity. And most recently, you read about authenticity, social purpose, and courage.

We've covered *a lot* of topics in this book. And all of them are especially curated to give you a competitive advantage in your career. Everyone's career path is different. We can't predict what the next three years will look like, let alone an entire career. The only certainty you have is that your future is within your control to shape as you wish. Your investment in your skills and knowledge will be pillars on which you can confidently stand—ready to adapt to the changing world ahead.

My intention with writing this book was to pass on the wisdom and insights from the top minds in business today. You will continue learning and developing your skills, and then relearn the lessons of this book in new and different ways.

You'll find that navigating an ambiguous career becomes easier as you mature. And with the knowledge you've acquired from this book, you will now be among the top performers who navigate their careers effortlessly *today*.

Luckily, many companies today are looking for people like you—a leader who can learn quickly and adapt.

With an uncertain future, companies are desperately looking to reskill their workforce to adapt to changing conditions. According to PwC's latest CEO survey, 38 percent of CEOs globally say they're extremely concerned about the availability of key skills as a threat to business growth.[26]

"To meet the promise of this age, mid-career upskilling

---

26 PwC, "Your Workforce Needs Reskilling," January 2018, https://www.pwc.com/us/en/services/hr-management/library/workforce-reskilling.html.

EPILOGUE

and transition must be a critical focus for both companies and individuals now," PwC says.

The World Economic Forum estimates that a third of primary core skills will need to shift in the near future for businesses to be successful.[27]

While this book provides you with the wisdom for social and interpersonal skills, determining the technical skills is up to you. Chase whatever excites you.

And here you stand, ready to fill the void that is left by the inactivity of others. All you need to do now is step up and live the career you've always wanted.

---

[27] PwC, "Your Workforce Needs Reskilling," January 2018, https://www.pwc.com/us/en/services/hr-management/library/workforce-reskilling.html.

Made in United States
North Haven, CT
04 January 2024

47045534R00098